Copyright © 2016 George Smith.

All rights reserved. No part of this publication may be reproduced, distributed or transmitted in any form or by any means, including photocopying, recording, or other electronic or mechanical methods, without the prior written permission of the publisher, except in the case of brief quotations embodied in critical reviews and certain other non-commercial uses peright law. For permission requests, write to the publisher:

Trademarked names appear throughout this book. Rather than use a trademark symbol with every occurrence of a trademarked name, names are used in an editorial fashion, with no intention of infringement of the respective owner's trademark. The information in this book is distributed on an "as is" basis, without warranty. Although every precaution has been taken in the preparation of this work, neither the author nor the publisher shall have any liability to any person or entity with respect to any loss or damage caused or alleged to be caused directly or indirectly by the information contained in this book

Part 1: The first steps	**3**
1.1 Choosing a puppy	3
Breeder or shelter?	3
Health and genetics	5
Breed characteristics	6
1.2 Before you bring your puppy home	8
What to expect from your new puppy	8
Supplies you will need	9
Preparing your home	11
1.3 The first day	12
Starting off on the right foot	12
Punishment and Reward	14
Discipline and rules	16
The Vet – vaccines, microchips, and neutering.	19
Part 2: A healthy, happy dog.	**20**
2.1 Potty Training	20
Absolute rules you have to follow	21
How to start potty training	21
5+ hours alone during the day	22
Going potty at night	22
What to expect from a normal day	24
2.2 Obedience	24
1. Paying attention	25
2. Sit and Down	27
3. Stay	28
4. Recall	28

5. Bonus tricks	29
2.3 Leash Walking	30
2.4 Socialization	32
2.5 Grooming	34
Oral Hygiene	34
Nail cutting	35
Fur care	36
Other puppy care tips	36
2.6 Nutrition	37
Part 3. Preventing and Correcting problems	**39**
3.1 Redirecting, Reinforcing, Exercising	39
Redirecting	39
Reinforcing	40
Exercising	41
3.2 Unwanted biting and chewing	42
3.3 Chasing	44
Leave it	45
2.4 Aggression and reading body language	46
3.5 Shy, reactive, and fearful dogs	49
Look at it	50
Confidence gaining for fearful dogs	51
Tug-of-war	51
3.6 Separation anxiety	52
What separation anxiety is	52
What causes separation anxiety?	54
What can you do about separation anxiety?	54

Final thoughts 56

Part 1: The first steps

So you've decided to embark on the exciting journey of dog ownership? Good for you! Having a dog in your life, when done right, is one of the most exciting experiences in the world. You will find great rewards, amazing insight, and lots of happiness all rolled up into one furry bundle. However, like most adventures, it's not something you want to embark upon lightly. A little bit of knowledge and preparation is going to save you a lot of trouble and heartache in the long run!

This book is designed to prepare you for your new life with your new puppy. It contains tips on what you need to buy and how to puppy-proof your house, exercises and games, and tons of advice for solving and preventing problems. Follow this advice and your puppy will have an excellent first year in your home – and you will have an excellent new puppy.

1.1 Choosing a puppy

Breeder or shelter?

The first thing you need to consider is whether you're going to get your puppy from a reputable breeder or look into shelters and foster homes in your area. There are arguments to be made for both cases, and we're going to look at why you would choose one over the other. Before going into that, though, there's one important thing you need to do no matter which path you take: make sure you are dealing with reputable professionals that work in full respect of the animals, the law, and health and safety regulations.

Whether it's a shelter or a breeder that you're looking for, it's always a good idea to ask for information from your local vet, kennel club or training center. They will have had contact with most of the breeders in the area and will be able to advise you on which to speak to and which to avoid. Once you have a few names, look them up online. Whether or not they have a website doesn't necessarily determine quality, but you might be able to find reviews about them. Don't be swayed by one good or bad review, but if there are lots of them, trust that they're there for a reason. Be especially wary of any breeder or shelter that has articles written about them online as having been abusive or neglectful. You would think that a place like that couldn't possibly stay open, but they sometimes do.

If you're looking at a breeder, look for one that specializes in your breed of choice. Most good breeders will only handle one or two breeds. Avoid the ones that claim they can get you any breed of puppy like the plague – they mostly source from puppy mills and disadvantaged countries. They should, by default, offer you all the proper documentation both for your dog and the transaction, and ensure that everything is completely above-board legally. Your breed dog bought from a breeder must absolutely come with a pedigree and a traceable genealogy. Apart from that, look for people that are helpful and forthcoming. Great breeders offer you detailed instructions on how to care for your new puppy, as well as some tools and supplies to start you off.

If you're looking at shelters, the main thing is to be sure that you're dealing with people that do their best to treat all of their charges with kindness. Shelters should be clean and happy places. If they are keeping puppies in bad conditions, in dirty kennels or in the cold, or if the puppies look ill and under-fed, run away. In these cases, it is also your moral obligation to immediately report what you have seen. Puppies that come from shelters should be vaccinated, micro-chipped, and in most cases, spayed or neutered. Don't even consider a shelter that lets you adopt a puppy who has never seen a veterinarian in his life. It's also great if you can find a shelter that treats you nicely and doesn't impose unreasonable conditions. They can ask to see your residence, which is perfectly normal, but if they want to make weekly house calls for the next five years you might want to avoid them.

Finally, how do you decide between getting your puppy from a breeder or a shelter? It's quite simple actually. You absolutely need to go to a breeder if:

- You want to participate in canine beauty shows

- You want to compete in any canine sports at a semi-professional or professional level

- You want to breed your dog further

- You want your dog to do a specific job that they were designed for: hunting, shepherding, home defense, sled pulling, etc.

- You are dead set on getting a specific breed and absolutely nothing can change your mind.

In every other condition aside from those above, you would do much better to consider adopting a puppy from a shelter or foster home.

Going to a breeder comes with advantages and disadvantages. The major advantage is that you know exactly what dog you are getting, what their health risks are, and what their family tree looks like. You can more or less tell the temperament of your future dog by looking at his ancestors. You will have a purebred dog with all the documents to testify to that, so you are free to participate in competitions or to breed it further. The disadvantages are that depending on the breed, it can cost you a lot of money. Not only will you pay a hefty sum for your puppy, but pure-bred dogs are also much more predisposed to genetic diseases which you will have to address with the help of a veterinarian.

Going to a shelter also has pros and cons. On the downside, your puppy will most likely be a strange mix of breeds and you won't know for sure what they are like until they grow up. However, this comes with the benefit of added health and resilience: mixed breed dogs tend to be much healthier and longer-lived. One immense advantage to getting a dog from a foster home is that they will very likely already be trained in the basics: walking on a leash and going potty outside at the very least. That can save you a lot of trouble. The greatest disadvantage is that your dog won't have a pedigree, and therefore can never take part in official competitions and shouldn't have offspring. Most of them can't since they are spayed or neutered as soon as they reach the shelter. However, if those things don't interest you anyway, then you should absolutely do a good deed and adopt a puppy that needs a home. Shelter dogs make the most intelligent, loving and rewarding pets.

Health and genetics

It's never easy to choose a puppy. Sometimes being faced with a litter of seven adorable bundles, or a shelter of dozens of wonderful dogs can be overwhelming. In the end, it's very likely that your heart will be the deciding factor in which puppy comes home with you. However, it's always a good idea to keep a couple of factors in mind, just in case you need a little extra help deciding. The important things you need to consider are genetics – in the form of health issues and breed characteristics. Let's take a look at the possibilities and why they matter.

Genetics can tell you a lot about what kind of dog your future puppy is going to grow up to be. Most importantly, people look at genetics in order to understand the potential health risks that a dog might be prone to, as well as their life expectancy and grooming needs. While breeders do their best to screen for breed-specific genetic diseases, many diseases don't actually have screening tests available. What's more, some of them occur based on complex factors, due to multiple genes as well as environmental conditions. This makes some genetic problems inevitable, and breeders should carefully screen all future breeding dogs for any signs of them – but they often don't. For example, tiny breeds like the Pomeranian and the Chihuahua are prone to Patellar Luxation – a painful disease in which the knee pops out of its socket. This could be selectively bred out of these breeds, and yet it's still very common. Part of the problem is that these dogs tend to be lap and purse dogs so this issue can go unnoticed for a very long time. The other problem is that some breeders focus much more on beauty than they do on health.

If you are considering getting a particular breed, it's a good idea to do some deep research into every single genetic disease which might affect that breed. Don't let these problems frighten you off from getting a dog, but do stay informed as to the possibilities and preventative measures you can take.

Here are the most common genetic diseases that dogs suffer from. No matter what breeds you're looking at, you're likely at risk from one or two of these.

- Heart problems

Many dogs can suffer from heart problems, but the most common congenital heart disease is Mitral Valve disease. It affects very small dogs, toy breeds and older dogs, and is quite lethal. It's common in dogs such as the Cavalier King Charles Spaniel. Dogs who have this problem may die due to congestive heart failure. It's very hard to identify this disease before it's too late, but you can get a good idea of your chances by looking at your puppy's ancestors, and all of his family members who are above the age of 7.

- Breathing difficulties

Scientifically called Brachycephalic Obstructive Airway Syndrome, this is a breathing problem characteristic of all brachycephalic dogs, aka dogs with very short snouts. This is one of the most controversial problems because it could be completely avoided by breeding against it. However, many people still consider shorter, flatter shouts on dogs such as the French Bulldog a "feature" and not a "problem", and breed for those visual aesthetics to the extreme. Their cute, button snouts can actually be the cause of heat stroke, asphyxiation, a collapsed trachea, and many other problems. You should be very well informed about how to handle a brachycephalic dog before buying it. Breeds that suffer from it are easily identified – they are every breed that has a flat face with a short snout.

- Allergies

This is a very common problem, albeit not the most severe. If treated and kept under control, not only is it not life-threatening, it can also be unnoticeable. There are many manifestations, the most common being skin reactions such as itchiness, hot spots, and ear infections. You're very likely to run into these if you're thinking about getting a Labrador or a Golden Retriever. They have over 40% chance of suffering from these to various degrees.

- Hip dysplasia

You've probably heard of this one, as it's quite a serious problem. It may not be life-threatening, but it does cause your pet severe pain and really limits their enjoyment of life. This disease can actually affect mix-breed dogs as easily as pure-bred dogs, and an estimate of 15% of all dogs suffer from it to some extent. Infamously, this is one to watch out for in German Shepherds and any breed that has a rounded backside. Smaller, square dogs with straight spines such as terriers tend to develop it much less frequently.

- Knee and ligament problems

Ligament ruptures and luxation of the knee are problems that you can find very frequently in Terrier breeds. Ligament rupture is, of course, a traumatic injury, but studies have shown that there is an increased risk for certain breeds due to the development of weak spots in their tendons. Many Terriers, as well as Rottweilers and Golden Retrievers, are at risk from this unpleasant rupture. Knee problems are very complex and sometimes difficult to identify, and they most frequently affect Terriers, Pomeranian dogs and Chihuahuas.

- Various other diseases

Things you might want to look out for include hereditary cancers and cataracts, as well as hypothyroidism and retained testicles. When in doubt, ask your local breeder or vet about what you can expect from each breed. Even if you're adopting a mixed-breed dog, look at his general body type and size. Is his snout short? Is his backside rounded? Is he tiny, or enormous? These things can tell you a lot about what sort of medical issues you might run into.

Breed characteristics

So what about breed characteristics? What else can we learn from the genetic background of our future puppy? Well, as it turns out, the genetic inheritance of each breed can tell us a lot about what we can expect from our dog. It can give us a rough idea of his needs in terms of exercise and companionship, of his particular strengths and weaknesses, of his attitude towards other dogs or people. There's a world of information you can find out, and it will do you a world of good to listen to it very carefully. Most dogs end up in shelters because their owners were hoping for a quiet couch potato and instead got a natural born killing machine. Their excuse? "we wanted a small dog!".

Breeds can roughly be grouped into a few categories based on the job that they were meant to do. Dogs within each category share a lot of characteristics in common, especially personality traits. By knowing what job your puppy is designed for, you will know what you can expect from him and what he expects from you.

The first major group you probably already know about is "companion dogs". Companion dogs are exactly what they sound like: dogs which were designed for no other purpose than to keep you and your family company. These are dogs that you shouldn't, and probably couldn't, convince to participate in sports or intense activities. They are most likely to be your classic couch potato, and many of them are portable purse dogs. This category includes French Bulldogs, Poodles, Chihuahuas, English Spaniels, Pekingese dogs,

Bichon dogs, Chinese Crested dogs, and many others. While they are quite companionable, they don't excel in intelligence and may not take much to games or training. They also won't give you very much trouble and need just enough exercise to stay fit and healthy.

Dogs that fall into the "Herding" group make amazing family pets. They are designed to work closely with people, and function very well in the context of a large family group or mixed pack. You can expect a herding dog to have a lot of energy and intelligence. You can also expect them to nip at your heels when they're young. They learn obedience better than any other group and are also quite adept at tricks and games. Some of the most skilled obedience dogs are German Shepherds, for example. They are going to need a lot more of your time though, especially the high-strung, high-energy Border Collie or Australian Shepherd. You can't get away with a walk a day and hope for the best with these dogs. Unless you are ready to invest time in training, walks, and sports, you might end up with a bored and troublesome dog. Other dogs in this category include the workaholic Malinois, the beautiful Welsh Corgi, and the fluffy Old English Sheepdog.

The "Hunting" group is a particularly strange mixed bag. This group includes most dogs that were designed to accompany hunters during gun sports, but from there on they get separated into different classes: Hounds, Pointers, Setters & Spaniels, and Retrievers. Whether designed to show you where the prey is, or to bring the prey back after it's been shot, these intelligent dogs are sure to have one thing in common: amazing prey drive. They are meant to work in close companionship with their master, and often form the strongest bonds. However, most of them do require regular brisk exercise. They all have amazing instincts for woodlands and water and are a great group to consider if you're a hiker or swimmer. Popular dogs in this group are Golden retriever, Afghan Hound, Basset hound, English Setter, Field spaniel, German Pointer, and many others.

The most terrifying of the groups comes in the form of Terriers. The "Terrier" group contains a lot of attitude in very small packages, and are the dogs that most often get confused for "easy pets" because of their small size and independence. This is, however, completely wrong. This group should be avoided at all costs by novice dog owners who have little time and little inclination for sports. They are absolutely not recommended for houses with other pets, especially small ones, as they are born to kill everything that moves. It's also not a great idea to put a terrier in a family with very small children, as they can easily drive each other, and you, crazy. Their prey drive is incredible, and they are completely fearless and reckless. The only thing stronger than their instinct to kill is their determination. If you don't want your Terrier to run the house, you have to be even more determined. They are bred to hunt and kill vermin such as rats, birds, badgers, foxes, and anything else they can get their teeth on. Popular terriers include the infamous Jack Russell Terrier, the Bull Terrier, Irish Terrier, the Scottish Terrier, and the Welsh Terrier.

The final group contains a mixture of various breeds designed for specific jobs, and is simply called "The Working Group". This largely covers dogs that are bred for home defense, as well as sled pulling or water rescue dogs. The main thing they all have in common is that they can be very single-minded: they have a job, they like that job and they want to do that job. You will never stop a

Husky from pulling, a Portuguese Water Dog from throwing himself into a puddle, or a Rottweiler from defending the home. The importance-away for you is that you need to be very familiar with what each breed is designed to do, and expect them to do it. Working dogs need exercise and mental stimulation, and if left jobless can become destructive or even dangerous. When considering getting a working dog, think about the context. If you like having friends pop into your yard or home whenever they want, a Rottweiler may be a bad decision.

1.2 Before you bring your puppy home

So you've decided on a puppy, and are just waiting for him to be ready to join you. Excellent! This is the perfect time to stop, look around yourself, and honestly evaluate how prepared you really are. A new life in the house is going to be a huge disturbance to everybody and everything, so it's better if you know exactly what to expect ahead of time. There are lots of things you can do to prepare yourself, your family and your home, as well as lots of supplies you will need.

What to expect from your new puppy

Many first-time dog owners aren't really prepared for what a puppy entails. Many experienced owners are also surprised since it's very easy to forget those rough first six months in the joy of what comes after. Various breeds have various needs, but puppies all have one thing in common: they demand a lot of attention and time. Ideally, you would have at least one weekend, if not a whole week, in which you have nothing else to do other than acclimatize your new puppy. Schedule his arrival in such a way that you don't just dump him in the house and go to work since that can be very traumatizing for a young dog.

Consider the fact that he has just been removed from his family and from everything he has known for his entire life. You should expect him to take a week to adjust to his new environment. It's also reasonable to assume that there will be a lot of barking and whining in the beginning, so you should talk to any neighbors and smooth things over in advance.

Puppies do sleep quite a bit. You can expect several hour-long naps throughout the day, as well as a full night of sleep if you educate him properly. However, when they are not sleeping, puppies are extremely active, curious and energetic. If left to their own devices, they can cause massive amounts of trouble in one minute, and will never give you a moment of peace.

In terms of exercise, more is better. A tired puppy is a happy puppy and has a happy owner. You should prepare for two walks a day, morning and evening, when his energy levels are going to be at their highest. You will also need one to two hours of active play (fetch, tug, chase) distributed throughout the day, and an hour of obedience training divided into 10-minute sessions throughout the day. Don't be surprised if you don't get much done in those first few weeks.

While adult dogs do tend to mellow down with age, you will still need to put in almost the same amount of time. The difference is that adult dogs have much higher stamina so you can do fewer sessions that last longer. Instead of two short walks a day, you can have a nice hour-long walk in the morning and that will be fine. Add to that a good half hour of fetch and games, and you will satisfy most dogs.

Puppies also need a lot of company. Don't expect that you will be able to leave him alone for 8 hours straight on his third day. If you work, you have to consider either puppy daycare, bringing him with you, hiring someone to come feed and play with the puppy at lunchtime, or coming home during lunch hour yourself. A puppy left alone for that long can develop serious mental issues, as well as destroy most of the furniture in the house.

Supplies you will need

There are an enormous amount of tools, toys, and treats available for dogs. It can be overwhelming if you walk into the pet store without a list. Most first-time puppy owners are guilty of over-spending and over-buying gadgets that they will never use. The following is a complete, comprehensive list of those things which you are absolutely going to make use of sooner or later. While some can be bought along the way, it's a lot better to just get everything in place before the new puppy arrives.

1. A crate that is large enough to fit your future adult dog + a way to divide it down to the size of your puppy.

Rather than buying a small crate for your puppy and then buying another one later, be a smart shopper and get one sized for your future dog. You can always use a separator to make the space smaller so that it doesn't feel too intimidating for your new pup, and to prevent him from going potty inside it. A crate is an absolute life-saver. It is the one and only safe way to transport your dog in the car, it can make potty training and sleep training much easier, it provides him with a safe space to retreat to, and it can give you some peace of mind. Say you have an emergency, and the puppy has to stay with the vet or come with you in the car for many hours? He can stay in his crate. Say you spilled something dangerous on the floor and need to prevent him from touching it while you clean? He can stay in his crate. Crates can help with separation anxiety, visits to the vet, and a whole host of other problems. We will be using them frequently throughout the training exercises in this book, so you absolutely need one.

2. A good quality harness, collar, and leash.

The leash is self-explanatory. Avoid the plastic retractable ones as they tend to teach your dog the bad habit of pulling, which is not what you want unless you're getting a husky puppy. Get a nice strong, lightweight leash that is 1.5 meters long. You should get both a harness and a collar, regardless of which you will choose to use with your dog when he is an adult. With a puppy, you have to use the harness for at least six months while he's still just barely learning to walk by your side. Even after that, it can be a great training tool, and useful for holding a puppy still during vet and groomer visits. You should also get a collar and keep it on your puppy at all times when outside, even though the leash will be attached to the harness. The collar should have an ID tag with your phone number on it so that if the worst should happen and your puppy escapes from his harness, anyone who finds him can call you right away. A collar is also a training tool you will use a lot in the future, so have a good quality, preferably leather one. It should be flat and have an adjustable size. Initially, it should fit on your puppy's neck snugly enough that you can put one finger under it comfortably, no more than that.

3. Bowls, food and hygiene products.

Buy two stainless steel bowls for food and water. Be sure to wash these regularly even if they seem clean. Buy enough good quality puppy food to last you a month, preferably the same variety that the breeder was using if possible. It's also a good idea to invest in some delicious healthy treats such as freeze-dried liver or heart. We will talk more about nutrition later in this book, but for now, just remember that most treats are junk food and should not be used by any responsible dog parent. Consider your puppy's hygiene needs. Will he need a specific kind of brush for grooming? Get that. Buy a large bottle of a natural, hypoallergenic dog shampoo – don't be afraid to spend a bit more on this item, since you will be using very little of it and it will last you a very long time. If you intend to clip nails yourself, get a dog-specific nail clipper. You can also buy toothpaste and a toothbrush, but it will be much easier to finger brush at first. There is more information on grooming later on in the book, and it includes instructions on nail clipping and tooth brushing.

4. Toys.

Don't go crazy getting complex toys as puppies are only going to chew through them. You need a variety of very simple toys with different textures in order to find out what your dog likes best. A great pack to start with would be: a dog-safe rubber bouncy ball to play fetch with, a rope to play tug with, and something soft tied to a durable string for chasing games. Make sure that all of these toys will fit in your dog's mouth, but are not small enough that he could choke on them. The other important thing you need to invest in right now is chew toys. Each dog has different preferences, but they all like to chew, so unless you're willing to sacrifice your slippers or the couch, you need to offer alternatives. A good selection of chew toys should include a natural rawhide bone, an antler or some other hard natural bone, a medium strength Nylabone or similar toy, a medium strength rubber teething ring, and a puppy Kong. Absolutely avoid any toys which are stuffed, or which have squeakers. Rest assured that your puppy will have more than enough predatory and destructive drive without these added stimuli.

5. Other small essentials.

Depending on your local ordinances, you may have an obligation to have a muzzle with you at all times when you are walking the dog in public, even if it's just in your pocket. A cheap, soft textile muzzle will more than suffice for this purpose, and you can also use it whenever you visit the vet. Buy a large supply of doggy waste baggies, as you will likely be using them frequently. Invest in a good quality bottle of enzyme cleaner for when your puppy has accidents in the house, as none of your current cleaning supplies will get rid of the smell and your puppy will attempt to pee in the same spot again. Chlorine actually makes the problem worse rather than better, the only thing that works is an enzyme cleaning solution. Don't fall for the lure of bitter apple deterrent spray, good training and obedience is all you need. You can also buy bedding, but it's probably going to get destroyed more than once during the first few months so you're better off using towels and old sweaters if you have them. If you want your dog to pee outside, absolutely do not buy pee pads. It's much better to train him to go where you want him to from the very first day.

Preparing your home

Now that you have everything you need, and you know more or less what you can expect, it's time to puppy-proof the house. This doesn't have to be a painful process, but it will involve you getting used to keeping a tidy home as everything left lying about can be a target for misadventure.

The absolute most important thing you have to do is make sure that the entire house is safe for a puppy, even the areas where you don't think he will be allowed. Big wobbly items of furniture should be secured or removed. All power cables should be raised, hidden, or at the very least tied down when the other options aren't possible. Shoes and remote controls should have their own places, out of reach or behind closed doors. Anything that's valuable or very dear to you should be safely stowed above-puppy level. Take special care to not keep books or other documents at floor level. It might also be a good idea to put any expensive, well-loved carpets away for a while, and only take them back out in 6 to 8 months.

If you have a yard, check the fencing. If there's a gap that your puppy could squeeze through, he absolutely will. If you intend to let him play outside without your supervision, invest in some chicken wire to reinforce the inside of all of your fences until your dog has grown. It may not be pretty, but it's only temporary. Add a layer of chicken wire to the inside of any balconies or terraces that have large gaps a puppy could fall through.

This would be a good time to decide where the puppy will spend time when unsupervised. If you were thinking of setting him down in the living room and letting him run loose, think again. That's a recipe for trouble, destroyed furniture, anger, and a ruined relationship. Try to set aside space where he can spend time with absolutely no chance of destroying anything of yours. This safe space can be a small room, or a corner of the living room fenced off by a playpen. Playpens don't cost a lot of money and are well worth it for your peace of mind.

Place his crate – divided to be just the right size for him – in this puppy space, and put bedding inside it. A good trick is to put one of your dirty shirts in there for the puppy, as having your smell nearby will help keep him calm at night. Expect any bedding you place in here to potentially be destroyed. Set down his food and water bowls. He should have fresh water available at all times until dinnertime, and food only on a regular schedule.

His toys should be divided into two categories: the play toys, such as the ball, tug toy, chase toy, Frisbee, etc. which should be placed in a box well out of reach, and his chew toys: kong, bones, antlers, etc. which should be available to him in his playpen at all times. Don't ever take his chew toys away from him, he should be encouraged to have one in his mouth constantly. But don't ever leave him alone with a play toy. It will become a chew toy and be destroyed within minutes.

Finally, and most importantly, prepare your family members. Young children should receive special instructions on how to behave with the puppy. If you want to avoid trouble, bite wounds, visits to the ER and other catastrophes, children should be expressly forbidden from ever jumping on the dog, shouting at the dog, pulling his ears or tail, wrestling with him, picking him up or even running around him. The puppy is not a toy. As much as your children would love to pick him up and walk around the entire house with him in their arms, one stumble can lead to a broken paw and a permanently damaged dog. Avoid the scenario in which the puppy is tired, grumpy, has had a rough day and is being pestered by the kids while he's trying to sleep. This can easily turn into a nasty bite from even the most benevolent of puppies. Puppies have incredibly sharp teeth in order to make up for being small and weak, don't underestimate them.

Remember to instruct everyone in the family that any items left lying around on the floor where the puppy can reach them are fair game and will be destroyed. What's more, kid's toys are a choking hazard for dogs and should be very carefully put away. Decide on ground rules that you all agree on and have to keep. Will the puppy be allowed on the couch? On the bed? Who is responsible for feeding and training him? Where will he sleep? The rules only work if everyone in the family agrees to them, otherwise, your puppy will very quickly learn who to turn to when he wants special treatment.

Congratulations, you're done! Your house and family are now ready for the new puppy. You have all the supplies you could possibly need, and you have a plan for how to care for him. You're about to start a wonderful journey and experience your first day with your new best friend!

1.3 The first day

Starting off on the right foot

It's important to start off on the right foot with your new puppy from day one. The rules you set now are going to set you up for success later on, so you should already know exactly what they are. Don't allow your puppy to do anything that you don't want him to do for the rest of his life. At this early stage, habits form quickly. We've all seen those hilarious photos of Great Danes who think they are still puppies and insist on sleeping in their owner's lap, but it's not so funny when it happens to you.

While the first day is not about training, you do want to start getting your puppy used to his environment. Start by placing him in his designated potty area, and spending some time there. If you're lucky, having just gotten there from a long trip, he might decide to use the facilities. This would be a great time to break out the treats and throw him a party!

Throughout the day, every time you see your puppy unconsciously doing something good, such as going potty outside, sitting, checking our his crate, drinking from his bowl or chewing on one of his readily available chew toys, make a huge fuss about rewarding him. Praise, cuddle and give treats like there's no tomorrow! By doing just this, you're already setting yourself up for success.

Try not to overwhelm your puppy as soon as he gets home. Get family members to greet the puppy quietly, one at a time, and limit play sessions to 15 minutes. Puppies get tired quickly and need to take breaks often, and tired puppies get grumpy and mean. Try to do your regular daily activities around him as much as possible – cooking and eating dinner, for example. Feel free to put him in his crate for naps, but keep his crate nearby at all times so that he can be close to you. He just got separated from his family, so he needs the company! Imagine that he is a small alien and you are showing him what a day in the life of a human is all about. Everything you show him now is going to be one less thing to stress him out later!

When he meets new people, get them to give him treats. Make sure every interaction is a happy one so that he will get used to you, your family, your neighbors, and strangers. We hope to cultivate a puppy that is trusting and loving, not one that is afraid of people.

Have little play sessions throughout the day. It's a rule with dogs that while they are playing, they aren't stressed or afraid. Those feelings are mutually exclusive. By playing tug or chase you give him a chance to blow off steam and relax. If your puppy is refusing to play at all, it could be a sign that he is stressed out. Start by removing all other people from the equation – especially children. If the puppy tries to retreat from a game, kids are very likely to grab him and drag him back where he doesn't want to be. You have to prevent this from happening at all costs. A stressed, tired and angry puppy is very likely to develop negative associations with the cause of his stress – in this case, little people. An adult dog who is aggressive towards children is a huge problem and a possible cause for euthanasia, so don't give him the chance to grow annoyed with them now.

Take him out to his potty area often. Later on in the book, we have a step by step potty guide, but for now, just be prepared that you will have to take him out very often on the first few days. Unless you have specifically seen him go potty, watch him like a hawk. He should not have free range of the house. If you have seen him go, then you can relax for about two hours.

Make sure his sleeping arrangements for that first night are comfortable. It's going to be a nightmare for both of you, either way, so be prepared, but do your best to make it easier on him. Start, on day one, by getting him to sleep where you intend for him to sleep for the rest of his life, be it in a crate, on a bed in his playpen, in a different room, next to your bed or anywhere else. Remember, there is no such thing as "it's just this once" in dog language. Once he's on your bed, it will take massive amounts of effort to deprogram that.

Set your alarm to wake up at least twice during the night to take him out to potty. If he's whining and barking, take him out to the potty area, but don't let him do anything else – no playing, no jumping up on the bed, no cuddles. If he goes – good, if not, he has to go right back to his bed anyway. Be strong. Don't give in to complaining. It will take a few days for him to get used to sleeping alone, so be prepared to have a few rough nights ahead of you. Placing one of your dirty shirts in his bedding can help, that way he can smell that you are near.

Enjoy your first day. It will be rough, but it will get better!

Punishment and Reward

Rewarding your dog is as simple as it gets – though many people still manage to get it wrong. However punishment is a tricky issue – there are those who say it should never be done. That is only partially accurate. It should never be done in anger, aggressively or violently. The right kind of punishment given at the right time is one of the most powerful educational tools in your arsenal.

What kind of punishment is acceptable, then? There are two major kinds of punishment which you can apply to a dog. Either you are adding something to the equation, which is called "positive punishment", or you are removing something from the equation, which is called "negative punishment".

An example of positive punishment is that your puppy is about to start chewing on your favorite slipper. You go to him and firmly but calmly tell him "no". You just added your voice, tone, and presence to the situation. Once a dog understands the concept of "no", that will be enough positive punishment 99% of the time.

An example of negative punishment is that your puppy got too aggressive while he was playing with you and bit you – hard. You calmly pick him up and put him in his pen, where he has to stay in time-out for the next half an hour. You just denied him the freedom to roam around the house and play with you – that too is a form of punishment and a very potent one.

Of the two, negative punishment is surprisingly the most powerful, and at the same time has the least chance of scaring or upsetting your puppy. It's what we're going to use most of the time in order to transmit to our puppy that certain behavior is not acceptable. Here is an amazing exercise that you can play with your puppy starting from the first day that will already introduce to him (and you) the concepts of "yes", "no", reward and punishment.

Puppy's first reward and punishment exercise.

You're going to need your puppy, a comfortable carpet to sit on, and a large bagful of delicious treats. This exercise also works really well with your puppy's regular kibble if he's hungry (and they always are). Just substitute giving him a regular meal with this exercise, keeping track of how much kibble you give him.

Step 1. Get down on the floor. Your puppy is likely going to come to you and check you out immediately. If not, be patient. When he does give you his attention, say "yes" happily and give him a treat.

Step 2. Your puppy is likely paying attention to you now. If he drifts away, either be patient or make a little noise to get him to look at you. When he does, say "yes" and reward him again. If he keeps his attention on you without getting distracted, keep rewarding him. We are simply teaching the pup that we like it when he pays attention to us, and that whenever he heard the word "yes" good things happen.

Feel free to repeat the first two steps and leave it at that for the first few sessions. It may not seem like much, but teaching your puppy that it's good when he pays attention to you is a huge deal.

Step 3. When you feel ready, put a treat in your hand. Make sure he sees that you did it. Close your fist around that treat, and offer your closed fist to your puppy. Make sure he doesn't get the treat. This may hurt a little – puppies have very sharp teeth, and it's likely he's going to dig and claw at your hand to get to the treat. While he is doing this, gently and calmly say "no."

Step 4. Wait. Be patient. If he is still digging at your hand after a minute, gently and calmly say "no" again. Remember that at this point he doesn't know what it means so he won't respond to it. We are teaching him by using negative punishment – we are denying him access to the treat that he wants.

Step 5. If you are lucky, it will only take a few seconds for your puppy to give up digging at your hand. If you are very lucky, he will then look at you to figure out what's next. When he does that, say "yes", open your fist, give him the treat, and shower him in treats and praise like it's his birthday.

Repeat steps 3 to 5 multiple times. Take a break, then repeat them again after an hour. Sooner or later, depending on how smart your puppy is, he will understand that the treat only comes when he stops chewing your hand and looks at you. When you can tell that he got it and it only takes him a second to get there, celebrate!

You have just taught your puppy to pay attention to you, and more specifically, to pay attention to your face rather than your hand. You have just taught him that when you make the sound "no", the good thing doesn't happen. But when you make the sound "yes!" it does! These are the fundamental things that you will need moving forward.

Repeat this exercise often, and for a very long time. Don't assume that just because he got the idea of "yes" and "no" in this context, he will know them everywhere else. Don't start throwing them around expecting things to happen. These are just the fundamental building blocks that you will use to construct respect and understanding between yourself and your puppy.

<u>Other important first day occasions to start practicing reward and punishment.</u>

Aside from the above exercise, there will be many situations in which you can and should practice reward and punishment, starting with the very first day. You should be stalking your new puppy like a hawk, ready to take advantage of any situation in which you can educate him.

If you're lucky and he goes potty as soon as you get him in the yard, that's a huge milestone and should be rewarded heavily. For the next six months, every time he goes potty in the right place, you should throw him a party. Praise is good, but treats are better, so have them on hand or stash them safely in the yard where you can reach them.

If you have an excitable pup who goes nuts whenever you're about to open the door or to set the food bowl down, practice negative punishment by making him wait. You're essentially saying "no, you don't get this thing that you want until you calm down." When he is no longer jumping up on the door or on you, you can reward him by doing what he wanted: opening the door or setting down the food bowl.

A word of warning: you have to be very patient and very careful. If you give him what he wants while he is still acting badly, you are going to reinforce his belief that that's the right way to behave.

For example: You are on the couch. The puppy is on the floor but wants to join you. He starts barking and whining.

What you should NEVER do: Go "ok, fine, just as long as you shut up." and pick him up on the couch. You will end up with a dog that barks at you and orders you around whenever he wants anything at all, and this could potentially escalate into dangerous, aggressive behavior.

What you should do: Pretend he's invisible as long as he's barking. Be patient. Wait for an hour, if that's what it takes. If you do anything to shut him up right now, you are going to get much worse barking later. When he finally stops and settles down, you can pick him up.

Another great way to use negative punishment is to enforce a time-out. This is especially useful for puppies which tend to play too rough or bite too hard. Whenever he becomes too excited and can't be calmed down, give him a five-minute time-out in his playpen or crate. By denying him the right to continue playtime, you are punishing him for going overboard.

These are all actions that will build up to solid foundations in the long run. They are not quick fixes, and one time-out will not make your hyper puppy permanently calm. But there is no such thing as a quick-fix for good behavior. Invest in your puppy's education now and you won't regret it when you have a loving, patient, calm, well-behaved adult dog.

Discipline and rules

Now that you know the "how" of enforcing discipline, it's time to talk about what exactly discipline is going to mean to you and your dog. When we say "discipline", most people think of army uniforms, black boots, waking up at 5 in the morning and shouting. But this isn't about giving your puppy, or yourself, a hard time. This is about setting rules and boundaries in such a way that you can develop a happy relationship without the risk of misunderstandings, anger, and trauma.

While it's nice to remember that our puppies are related to magnificent wild animals such as wolves and jackals, it is also important to remember that they are only very distantly related. Our pups have been bred for thousands of years to be what they are, from the moment the first wolf took a piece of fried meat from the first hunter. They are designed to live with us, work with us, and most importantly, to cooperate with us. A dog that does not have a role in the family does not know his place and does not have a job is an unhappy, unsatisfied dog.

You may have seen the classic case of the Jack Russel Terrier who thinks he is the owner of the house. He attacks visitors, barks at the television, demands to sleep on his owner's pillow and growls if you go near his toy. Some people would say he is only being a dog, doing what is naturally his instinct to do. That's absolutely wrong. A dog living under those conditions is constantly stressed out and miserable. He doesn't feel safe in his own family, because there's nobody there to take charge – so he has to do it. Even though he doesn't like it.

A dog that does not live under a framework of discipline is always an unhappy dog. No matter how kind-hearted you are and how adorable your puppy is, you have to remember that you need to do the hard work for his well being and for the well being of your family. We have no doubts that discipline and education are quintessential for young children, and yet many puppy owners assume that the same isn't true for puppies. Complete freedom is a recipe for disaster in both cases, but by setting reasonable rules and maintaining discipline you can have a happy and balanced household.

The actual rules change from case to case, from owner to owner. Nobody has the right to tell you what you are or are not allowed to do with your own dog. Behaviors that are acceptable to some families may not be acceptable to others. Whatever you choose, you're the one who is going to have to live with it. There are some universal rules, and there are some that you will have to decide for yourself. In both cases, the time to start enforcing them is now, on day one. Don't allow your puppy to do things that you don't intend to allow him forever. Dogs don't understand the concept of "it's a special occasion" or "it's just until he grows up."

Universal rules for a disciplined puppy

1. It is never ok for the puppy to bark, bite, whine or growl to get what he wants. Ever. This is an immediate cause for negative punishment. This includes begging for food, toys, treats, coming up on the couch, or even just getting your attention. Never give in to puppy manipulation. Reward calm, civilized behavior only. The one exception? If he's whining at the door because he needs to pee. That's usually considered a great thing!

2. It is never ok for the puppy to chew objects other than his designated, puppy-safe chews. Remove the object in question

immediately, replace it with an appropriate toy, and praise him for chewing on his toys.

3. It is never ok for the puppy to attack other people or dogs, not even if he's "jealous" because you are interacting with them and not him. It's not cute, it's dangerous behavior. This should be cause for an immediate time-out.

4. It is never ok for the puppy to decide when and how much he eats. It doesn't matter if he looks like he's always hungry, you know better. Most puppies will eat until they vomit if allowed. There's a chapter later on about nutrition and obesity, it will help you figure out how much food he needs. Stick to that measurement. Don't ever allow a puppy to bully you into putting down a bowl of food. Wait until he is calm and do it on your own terms.

5. A disciplined puppy must allow you to touch him. This includes his paws, his belly, his tail, looking inside his ears, opening his mouth and looking at his teeth. This is not something that will just happen overnight: you have to take the time to do it, a little at a time, every single day until it becomes completely natural. You have to be able to groom your puppy, check for injuries, check his dental health, administer medication, and lots of other things. If you can't touch him, you can't help him when he needs it, so this rule really isn't up for debate.

Personal rules that you get to decide

1. Where will he be sleeping? The best possible option would be a comfortable, correctly sized crate. Even if he complains at first, adult

dogs love having their den to which they can retreat to get some peace and quiet. Second best would be a doggie bed. You can place it inside his play-pen to still have some control at night – not as much as a crate gives you, but enough. Worst on the list would be your bed. This may still work for shy, submissive dogs but it's an absolute nightmare if your dog happens to be stubborn and dominant. He could easily decide that because he sleeps next to you he is just as important as you in the pack, or more so. And you won't really know that until it's too late.

2. Where is his potty area? Most people recommend outside on the grass. Depending on your situation and your pup, puppy pads are not completely to be excluded. They could be a fine option in an apartment, in a high-rise, for a companion type breed. Wherever it is, pick one and stick to it.

3. Who will be the primary trainer and educator of the puppy? Of course, a disciplined dog will obey anyone in the family, but there should always be one person who gets the final word. Think of this scenario: you are out with your family and puppy. He wiggles out of his harness and starts gunning it for the road. Cars are passing at high speed. You all panic. Some of your family members yell "Stop!" others yell "Come here!" from three different directions. Your puppy needs to know, in a split second, whose voice is the one he actually obeys. It can be a matter of life and death.

4. Is he allowed up on the couch? The chairs? The table? The kitchen counter? No? Then don't ever allow him to even consider going on there. If he's been on it once, he will consider it his right to go there again. Is he allowed up on your lap? Consider this one wisely. Refusing to let a puppy sleep on your lap is one of the

hardest things a new dog owner can do, but when that puppy grows up and weighs more than you do, regrets quickly sink in.

5. What are your leash walking goals? Do you consider him well disciplined if he only pulls a little and then comes back? If he never reaches the end of the leash, but within that limit walks freely? Or will you only be satisfied if he walks in "heel" position all the time? While the "heel" position is harder to train, it is absolutely possible, and in some cases necessary – such as when being walked by an elderly person or a pregnant woman. Some dog breeds take to it more than others. Normally, moderation is best in these situations – the walk has to be fun for your dog too.

6. Where will he have access once the potty-training phase is complete? It's perfectly fine to keep some rooms as dog-free zones. It might be a great idea for the children's room, for example. Perhaps you want to keep him out of the second floor of the house. One thing should be very clear, however – if you intend to get a dog to keep exclusively in the yard, potentially tied to a dog-house, don't. That's not an acceptable life for any dog, and most countries are working on eliminating that primitive practice. Most shelters won't even let you adopt a dog unless you guarantee that it gets to be in the house, with the family.

It's a good idea to keep these rules in mind, or even write them down on paper. It's inevitable that some will change as your puppy grows older and you begin to understand what you expect from each other. However, you still need to start from somewhere, right from the first day.

Now that you know how to praise and punish your puppy, to teach him the foundations of the concepts of "yes" and "no", and what exactly your discipline goals are, you're ready to take your first few days head-on. There will be more detailed instructions for specific categories such as obedience or potty training later on, but they all use the same basic concepts that we've already explored in this section. Practice rewarding your puppy whenever he does something good, and finding an appropriate punishment when you don't like his behavior. Never punish him in anger. There's no point, you're only going to frighten him and ruin your relationship. Instead, be an educator and work with him towards your discipline goals.

The Vet – vaccines, microchips, and neutering.

Your final consideration for this big day is booking an appointment with your vet for a regular health check-up, as well as any planned future interventions such as vaccination. Depending on your situation and where your puppy comes from, he may (and should) already be vaccinated, micro-chipped, and potentially spayed or neutered. If he's not, this has to be done as soon as possible. Let's look at your options and obligations.

Finding a vet shouldn't be too hard. Most of the times, unless you have a specific reason to avoid him, your local town vet it a safe bet. Make sure he's nice, and make sure he's always available. He should have an emergency number for when he's off duty. If something happens to your pup in the middle of the night, he has to be available. It will cost you, but you need to have that option. Also, it might be a good idea to find a backup vet in case anything happens to your primary one.

Vaccines are mandatory in most places in the world, and for good reason. There are many horrible ways in which your puppy could get sick from viruses and bacteria, often passed to him by unvaccinated dogs through something as brief as a sniff. Some are carried by mosquitoes, ticks or fleas. There's no reason to take any chances as they cost very little, only need to be topped off once a year, and have absolutely no harmful side-effects. Don't fall for the hype: there's no such thing as over-vaccinating.

Most vets are going to give your puppy his first set of shots around 3 months of age, so book them now. They also recommend that you should avoid taking him out in public until they have had all of their shots, which can be as late as 6 months time, but that's actually impossible. You need to start on leash training and socialization. A dog that is separated from the world for the first 6 months of his life is going to be dysfunctional to a lesser or greater extent forever. One option is to use your yard if you have one, and invite friends over with dogs which you know are healthy and vaccinated. You could also take walks on quieter, more isolated streets. One thing is true, you should probably avoid large crowds as much as possible, and especially avoid meeting any stray dogs until you've had the full range of shots.

Micro-chipping is also mandatory in most countries, and even if it isn't, it's a good idea. Hundreds of dogs are rescued every day and sent back to their loving families thanks to being micro-chipped. Harnesses can break, tags can fall off, but that chip is forever. The procedure takes an instant, it hurts about as much as a bee sting (which your puppy will surely experience more than once in his life) and is completely safe. Many shelters offer help to people who can't afford the cost of the procedure, and some will even do it for free.

As for spaying or neutering, it tends to be a big debate but is really a very simple question. If you got your puppy at a shelter he's probably already neutered. It's standard procedure and has helped reduce the number of stray dogs in recent years more than any other practice. If he's not, the decision is ultimately yours, but here's a rough guideline:

- You absolutely have to do it if your dog has any sort of genetic disease or is at high risk for any sort of genetic disease. You have to do it if he needs it for health reasons – such as ovarian tumors.

- You don't have to, but still probably should do it if you don't know your dog's genetic background, and suspect it might be dubious. This is the case for most shelter dogs. You should also do it if your dog tends to be an escape artist, and you live in a community where most people don't spay or neuter, like most villages. The goal here is to avoid putting more unsound, unhealthy, unwanted puppies out into the world.

- You don't have to do it if you are sure that your dog is genetically sound, is secure on your property, and has zero health risks related to his reproductive organs.

- You absolutely must not do it if you intend to breed your dog or have him participate in any sports or breed competitions.

Remember that this is not about you and your pride. This is about what's best for your dog and for your community. If you have doubts about neutering your dog, just go visit the local shelter and see how many unwanted dogs are still in the world. Many shelters still have to kill the animals that don't get adopted quickly enough. What was the point of allowing that to happen?

As for the rumors that dogs become slow, fat and lazy after they get neutered: that's completely false. Yes, his dietary needs may change a little bit, and it's your job to adjust for that. An obese dog is the fault of the owner, not of neutering. If you keep your dog fit, healthy and active, he will remain fit, healthy and active his whole life. The evidence that dogs "calm down" after neutering is circumstantial: Most dogs are neutered between 6 months and 1 year of age. That's roughly around when they would naturally start to calm down no matter what you do to them. It's part of the process of growing up. That's also why neutering is never a solution to a hyperactive, aggressive pet. It won't even stop him from humping your leg. The only thing it changes is his ability to create unwanted puppies destined for the shelter.

Part 2: A healthy, happy dog.

2.1 Potty Training

It's a good idea to start thinking about potty training as soon as your new puppy walks in the door. It may not be as life-saving as a good recall, or as fun to show to your friends as a solid roll over, but going potty is going to be a big deal to the both of you, so you should know how to do it right.

Potty training is the one part of your dog's education that will take the longest time before showing any result at all, and often times it can seem like you're taking more steps backward than forward. Most owners go through several bottles of enzyme cleaner and multiple carpets before they can breathe a sigh of relief – and that only comes around the time your puppy is one year old. However, if you don't take steps towards teaching your dog when and where to go potty, it won't come at all. So let's get started!

Absolute rules you have to follow

- Clean all potty "accidents" with enzyme cleaner only. Absolutely no bleach or household cleaners, they will only make matters worse.

- If you discover an "accident" after it's already been done, do not punish your puppy. This is extremely important. Bringing your puppy to the scene of the crime, shouting, showing him what he did will absolutely NOT work. You will damage your relationship, hurt the puppy and achieve nothing. Clean the area carefully and move on. This rule is firm. If you can't obey it, you might as well invest in puppy diapers because you're going to be here for a very long time.

- If you catch your puppy in the middle of "going" on the carpet, remove him calmly and without anger to his designated potty area. Do not shout, do not shake the puppy, do not punish him in any way. You are an educator, not a source of danger for your puppy.

- If you catch your puppy "going" in the right place, you must reward him heavily. Keep his treats handy at all times, stash some in your pockets, stash some near his potty place. Don't get caught without treats.

- Do not purposefully allow your puppy to go potty in the wrong place. Many owners think they can get away with letting him potty indoors while they are at work but teaching him to go outdoors the rest of the time. Or letting him go indoors "just until he grows up". This will not work. You have to make alternative arrangements for when you are away. There should only be one correct potty place, and he should always use that place.

How to start potty training

We've already talked about this but it bears repeating: as soon as you bring your new puppy home, bring him to his potty area first before anything else happens. Let him hang out there with no distractions for a bit. With a bit of luck, you will have your first chance to reward him right away!

The system is very simple from then onward. You have to watch your puppy like a hawk. Soon you will start to recognize his patterns: sniffing the ground, heading for corners or carpets, circling around the same spot a few times. If you manage to catch him in time, take him out to his potty spot and praise his success!

Now that you're sure your puppy just went potty, you can breathe a sigh of relief and maybe let him play by himself, chew a bone, or hang out in his playpen for an hour or two. After that, you have to go back to watching him like a hawk! You can expect your puppy to need to pee once every three to five hours, depending on his size. If he's eating the right food, in the right quantity and of the right quality, he should be pooping as many times a day as he is eating – most commonly that will be twice a day. The good thing about puppies is that usually, when food goes in, within the next 10 minutes, they will also need to poop. This gives you a lot of control over making sure that he goes where you want him to.

You can't leave a puppy by himself for more than a few hours for the first month of his life with you. Not if you want to educate him quickly and efficiently. If there's nobody at home while you're at work, be prepared to ask or hire someone to stop by for a potty and play break once or twice a day.

5+ hours alone during the day

It's not ideal, but it's a situation that realistically can happen. Everyone in your family works full-time, and you can't find anyone to visit him this week, and there's no puppy daycare in your area, and none of your friends like puppies. Aside from needing new friends, you're also going to need some sort of solution for him to go potty while you're away.

In these situations, a puppy playpen is absolutely mandatory. A crate is too restrictive, and having free roam of the house has too many variables, so you need to place him in a playpen where he has access to his bed, water, chew toys, and a potty area.

This potty area has to fulfill two requirements: it has to be on the opposite side of the pen from his bed, as he will try to "go" as far away from his bed as possible. And it has to be made of the same material as his normal potty area.

If you normally want him to go outside on the grass, you're in luck! You can easily set up a potty system for him indoors by filling a plastic or disposable aluminum tray with litter or puppy pee pads and covering it with a large enough square of either turf or fake grass. You can get everything you need in any home improvement store cheaply. The same goes for gravel-going puppies! Cover the litter or puppy pee pads with the same gravel you have outside in his potty area.

It's really not a good idea to use just plain puppy pee pads or newspapers. Once a dog gets used to a certain sound and texture, he will always want to use the same one. It's much better to start off with the right texture from day one.

Going potty at night

Puppies have small bladders. Even the largest of breeds will still need to go out once or twice during the night. Normally this lasts up until around six months of age, but it varies from puppy to puppy and breed to breed.

The absolute best thing to do is to train him to sleep in a crate at night. Dogs are den animals, and they have the instinct to never soil where they sleep if they can help it. The space he has in his crate should be just enough for him to stand up, sit, lie down and curl up. If the crate is any larger than that, you will have to divide it into smaller sections. It's not meant to be a luxury villa, just a bed for the night.

Crate training your puppy has hundreds of advantages, including helping you potty train. While he's young, you will have to close the door to the crate at night so that he has to vocalize and ask you when he needs to go potty. When they are older, crate-trained dogs love to go sleep in their safe, snug crates at night and you can even leave the door open for them. Once they have these good habits ingrained, they never lose them!

Teach your puppy to love his crate slowly by rewarding him for each step. Throw treats inside and let him chase them. Have him sit inside and reward him through the door. Let him come back out, throw a toy inside and reward him for chasing it. In short, make him feel completely comfortable about his crate. Only close the door for a few seconds and reward him again. Take it slowly and make him think that his crate is the best place on earth!

In the evening, remove his water bowl right after dinner. If he keeps drinking right until he goes to bed, you will end up getting up much more often than you'd like. He will not become dehydrated if he doesn't have any water available between 7 p.m. and 7 a.m.! When you are ready to go to bed, take him to his crate and throw some treats and a delicious chewy toy inside. With luck, he will be so thrilled by the bedding and so eager to chew he won't even notice you closing the door.

If he whines right away, don't give in. Of course, he would rather be sleeping on the bed, on your pillow, but that's not where a good puppy belongs. Don't give in to him manipulating you and complaining. If you open that crate door even once while he's whining, he will immediately understand that whining makes you open the door and he will never stop doing it.

However, it's very important that you keep the crate somewhere where you can hear him during the night. If he settles down, falls asleep, and then wakes up and cries, that's a sure sign that he has to go right away! Take him to his potty area and praise him wildly if he uses the facilities. Then take him right back to his crate.

Even if he doesn't cry out, it's a good idea to set your alarm clock to wake you up twice during the first few nights and take him out. If you notice that he seems happy to go only once and then sleep through the rest of the night, adjust your alarm accordingly. If you're lucky, within a week or two, it's even possible that going once very late right before bed and once very early in the morning will be enough!

Adult dogs can easily hold it for an entire night with no problem, and if they're well educated to sleep in their crate and go potty outside you will never have to worry about a thing.

What to expect from a normal day

Once you start to get into the rhythm of when your puppy needs to go, it will become second nature to you. Here's a rough schedule of when you can expect an average puppy, say age 5 months, to need to go potty if you follow our system and he's learned what's expected of him:

- As soon as you wake up in the morning, before anything else, potty break

- Breakfast at the same hour each morning, and another potty break 5 to 15 minutes after

- If the puppy is "empty", relax for a few hours

- Around 5 months, you can expect a potty break every 3 to 4 hours

- Dinner at the same hour each day, a potty break 5 to 15 minutes after. Remove water bowl

- Last potty break before going to bed, say 10 p.m.

- One potty break during the night, say 3 p.m.

It may seem like quite a bit at first, but having a puppy is quite a huge commitment. This schedule can and should be divided among multiple people, including yourself, your family, your neighbors, a professional dog sitter/walker, a puppy daycare, or friends who want to help. Unless you work from home, it won't be possible to properly potty train your puppy.

Of course, if you can't do this, it's not the end of the world. Your puppy may learn to go outside long before being 6 months old with the right care, or it may take him two years if you don't have the time. Follow this advice as much as you possibly can for both your benefit, but don't sweat it if accidents happen. Just keep a supply of enzyme cleaner handy, and sooner or later you will get there!

Potty training can be one of the most frustrating experiences for a new puppy owner. There are plenty of books and experts out there who are ready to tell you that if you have even one "accident" in the house, you have failed. Don't believe them, and don't let potty accidents ruin your relationship with your dog. Most sensible experts will admit that accidents happen, maybe even daily at first. As long as you're making some form of progress, you will get there sooner or later. A good way of keeping track is to put up a sign on your fridge that says "Days without an accident" and keep track of the number. Perhaps, at first, that number will be 0 for a long time. But sooner or later it will become 1, then 2; and before you know it, you will forget to update it.

2.2 Obedience

An obedient puppy is a well-integrated, happy member of his family. That is why basic obedience should be given top priority over the first few months of your puppy's life with you. It takes time and lots of repetitions, but the good news is that you can teach him the basics of puppy obedience within the first few days! Then it's up to you to repeat and enforce those behaviors in various situations, locations and at various times.

While discipline is more about the rules of the house, obedience is about specific interactions that you have with your dog in which you ask him to do something and he obeys you. At first, none of this will happen. Lots of dog owners say "oh, my dog doesn't even answer to his name". Your dog doesn't speak English! Unless you teach him, there is no way he can ever answer and obey you. Sure, there are some very rare dogs that figure some basics out on their own, but that's thanks to their intelligence, not your good communication.

When people talk about a puppy who is not at all obedient, they usually have these complaints in mind:

1. He does not listen to anything I say at all.

2. He does not come when called.

3. He does not respond to any of the position commands such as sit or down.

4. He does not respond to "stay".

5. He does not walk on a leash politely.

These five simple things are often the difference between a puppy which is loved and cared for, and one who ends up sent to the shelter or banished to the yard permanently. We will be taking a look at leash walking in the next chapter in much greater detail, but we can take care of the other four now, as well as show you a few other useful commands.

1. Paying attention

Before you can get to do any fancy tricks, you need your puppy to pay attention to you. Most of the time, you will set your puppy down in a room and he will immediately start to sniff around, chew on things, play with things, and generally ignore you.

It's a good idea to teach him that whenever you call his name, he should pay attention to you. You have to remember this rule carefully and not mix it up with his recall command, which will be "Name, come!". Just saying his name should get him to look at you, nothing more. For the purpose of this exercise, let's say his name is "Charlie".

You should take Charlie to a distraction-free space for this exercise. The yard is a bad idea, as birds and people and cats can all pass by and ruin your focus. A room with no toys or anything interesting in it would be ideal.

<u>Getting his attention - exercise</u>

Try sitting down on the floor. When your puppy is looking away, making himself busy, call our "Charlie" in your happiest voice. For many puppies, this might be enough to get him to look at you. If he does, you know what to do – say "yes", offer him treats, praise, and cuddles. Essentially throw him a puppy party.

If the sound of your voice isn't enough to get him to look at you, these extra tricks should help:

- Get lower and closer. Try to be as close to his level as possible, and no more than one meter away.

- Call him in a higher tone, while making silly waving motions with your hands. Puppies love playtime, so be playful.

- Add a little kiss noise or whistle after his name.

No matter how you get his attention, be sure that it's not by repeating his name a hundred times. Think of his name like a rechargeable phone battery. The more you abuse it, the more you will need to let it charge, so use it sparingly.

As soon as you get his attention in any way, reward him heavily. Then wait until he gets distracted. Call "Charlie" again. At this point, you will have a great indicator of how quickly your puppy learns and how much of a struggle training him will be. The brightest pups will already respond more quickly the second time around, having understood that "Charlie" means treats. Pups which are slower may take a hundred repetitions before they start to get the idea. Most dogs fall somewhere in between.

Your goal is that your pup learns that every time he hears his name, great things happen. His reward can be food, toys, games or cuddles. Whatever makes him happy will work!

When to practice it

Once he has the basic idea down, call his name whenever you have something good that you're about to give him. Call his name before he has his meals, even if he's already looking at you holding the bowl. Call his name before giving him a delicious treat. Any happy occasion should be a chance to call his name.

When to avoid it

Refrain from ever using his name right before something bad happens unless you want him to run away as soon as he hears it. Most dog owners make the mistake of scolding their dogs for bad behavior by using the phrase "Charlie, no! Bad dog!". Not only is that kind of scolding very ineffective, but it also creates negative connotations with his name that you really don't want to have.

How to advance it

So your puppy has figured it out, and every time you say "Charlie" he looks at you and wags his tail expectantly. How can you take this amazing new superpower further? The best thing would be to slowly increase the distance and the level of difficulty.

Call him from one meter, then two, then from across the room. Go outside in the yard, call him from one meter, then two, then across the yard. Get him to look at you while there's someone else in the room with you. Get him to look at you while someone else is playing with a ball, or while there's another dog present. Introduce all new steps very slowly, and as soon as one of them becomes too difficult, take a step back. If having another person nearby is too distracting, start with the person being far away. Invent your own ways of making it more difficult, but always give him the chance to learn slowly and set him up to win. You should never give him the chance to fail a command twice in a row!

2. Sit and Down

It may not seem like much now, but knowing sit and down can make a huge difference in how you manage your dog, especially in public situations. It's not about getting him to sit whenever you want it, it's about the fact that while he's sitting and paying attention to you he's much less likely to go chase whatever passes by.

You can take your dog with you anywhere you want (as long as it's permitted), for example, out for drinks in your local brewery with your friends, if you're certain that you can get him in "down" position, on his blanket, under the table. He can be with you in a crowded queue as long as he's willing to sit patiently by your side. Any time he's in "sit" or "down", it's much less likely that he's going to get up and go.

Sit

Sit is a great command because you can start teaching it right away. Most puppies will get the basic idea within ten minutes. Very smart puppies may start responding to the voice cue by the second day.

Start, as usual, in a distraction-free environment. Have a pocket full of treats, a hungry puppy, and a lot of patience. Take a treat in your hand and hold it tightly between your fingers. Place it close to your puppy's nose.

Now, imagine that the treat and the nose are magnets. You can move one to move the other, but you have to move slowly and keep them close to each other otherwise the effect wears off. This technique is called "luring".

Slowly lift the treat over his forehead and towards the back of his head. Don't go high up so that he has to jump to get it! Your goal is to get him to move his nose up and his head back. When his head goes backward, his butt will go down. As soon as this happens, let him have the treat and add a few more for good measure!

Repeat this step a few times. When you see that he starts to understand what you want, and puts his butt down automatically as soon as you pull out a treat, start saying "Sit" as he is sitting down.

You will have to repeat this exercise hundreds of times over many days before he responds to you saying "sit" without luring him into it. Then a few hundred more before he does it reliably without the treat! Always reward him for obeying you. If you ask him to do it and don't reward him, next time he might not do it.

<u>Down</u>

Use the same principle as for "Sit". When your puppy is sitting, give him a treat. Take another treat in your hand, place it close to his nose, and very very slowly move your hand in a straight line down. When you are halfway down, start also slowly pulling it slightly towards you. Your mission is to get your puppy to bow his head, then stretch out on his belly.

Because this is a harder position than "sit", at first you can reward even intermediate steps, such as following the treat down for a few inches. The first time he moves his front paws forward is also a major milestone. Try doing this on a soft carpeted surface to make it easier on him.

Once he starts to understand what you expect from him, which may take upwards of 20 repetitions, start saying the word "Down" as you are moving the treat downwards. Then repeat the exercise, including the word, as long as it takes for him to get it.

When your puppy begins to anticipate you and goes into "down" position without needing luring, you can start to give the command to him while standing, from a few steps away, or from across the room. This won't be easy, be prepared and expect it to take many months.

For now, don't expect your dog to stay in this position for a long time. That comes later when you've taught him "stay" and give him both commands together. Remember that "sit" and "down" are just positions, while "sit-stay" and "down – stay" include duration.

3. Stay

Once your puppy knows "down", you can easily add the command "stay". Catch him in a calm moment, you don't want to teach him this while he's bouncing off the walls! Instead of "luring", this time we have to rely on his intelligence.

When he is in "down" position, calmly but firmly say "Stay", show him your open palm making a "stop" gesture, and reward him. At first, he won't understand what happened – it was barely half a second between the command and the reward.

Next, repeat that but wait one second between saying "Stay" and rewarding him. If that works, count to three next time. Then count to five. If he gets up from his position, calmly say "no", lure him back into "down" and re-start from the one second "Stay".

Keep extending the time until you get to a count of 15. If he gets there successfully, you can start considering moving slightly. At first, make a vague gesture of standing up. If he doesn't move, reward him! Slowly build up to you getting up and taking one step back.

Each time your puppy moves, tell him "no" and restart the exercise. Make sure that the time after that you only give him so little time that he can't mess it up. If it looks like he's getting bored with the exercise, end the session and try again later! Most puppies can only work on "Stay" for a minute or two before getting bored.

4. Recall

This is the most important command in your arsenal because it could potentially save your puppy's life. It's vitally important that whenever you yell "Charlie, come!" Charlie comes running to you at full speed. Of course, you would substitute "Charlie" for your own pet's name!

The way to begin this is easy. Either use a friend to hold him in place using a harness and leash, or get him in a solid "down" and "stay" position. Walk away from him with your pockets full of treats and your hands full of toys. Yell "Charlie, come!" and jump up and down and throw toys around like you're the most interesting person in the world. If he's being restrained, have your friend release him at that moment. Watch him gallop towards you and enjoy! When he gets to you, throw him a big puppy party. Repeat this exercise many times throughout the day, and make sure that at the end of every single "Charlie, Come!" there's a huge reward.

Most owners complain that whenever they yell "Charlie, come!" Charlie either ignores them or runs off in the other direction. There's a very good reason why this happens: Once, when they called their puppy and he didn't come back, they eventually caught him and then scolded him or smacked him for not coming back sooner. It's understandable, you think a child would understand why he is being punished, so a dog would too, right? Wrong.

He just understood that when you call him, it's because he's about to get scolded, so he has absolutely no reason to come to you. He had no idea why he's being punished, he just knows that when he gets called back it's bad news.

The absolute most important rule you have to follow is that no matter how bad it gets, even if it takes him an hour to come back when he eventually does come back, you are not allowed to punish him in any way. On the contrary, you should reward him for coming at all, so that next time he will want to come back even sooner.

If you want to avoid having that problem at all, don't even consider trying to recall him when he's distracted. If you already know he's not coming back, because you lost him to a stray squirrel, for example, don't even try it. Go there yourself and bring him back. The more time you spend shouting "Come!" and having him not come, the more you train him that that's an acceptable outcome. Only use this command when you're sure it will be obeyed, and always reward it more than you think you should.

5. Bonus tricks

Any day you teach your puppy something new is a great day for him. While there are thousands of tricks and games he can learn, here are some of the easiest ones that you can work on right away. Perhaps not all of them are useful, but they will all make you and your friends smile.

Shake

A favorite of kids, shake is really easy to teach. Once you have your puppy in a firm "sit-stay", tickle the back of his paw very gently with your fingers. This will cause him to lift it slightly. When he does, say "yes" and reward him. After a few repetitions take a break. The next time you try him, keep tickling to get his paw to go even higher. When it reaches the right height, gently grab it in your hand and say "shake". Reward him profusely and keep repeating the exercise. They usually learn it in a matter of days!

Spin

Another very easy puppy trick, "spin" simply implies him doing a full 360-degree circle. Not to be confused with "rollover" which is a much more advanced trick. Using the technique of "luring", try to move your puppy around by keeping a treat close to his nose and moving your arm. When he seems confident that following the treat is what you want him to do, simply get him to move in a circle. As he completes the circle, say "spin" and reward. Repeat many times and soon your puppy will spin on command!

Reverse

A very useful trick, reverse is a great way to teach your puppy that he has a rear end. It may seem obvious to you, but very young puppies aren't quite aware of their tail ends and often just drag them around behind themselves. It takes time to become agile and aware of their entire body, and this exercise helps with that. Put a treat in your hand in such a way that your puppy can smell it, but not take it, and put your hand in front of your dog at his nose height. Then, slowly move your hand towards his tail in such a way that he has to back up to keep up with it. If he sits down, your hand is too high up. Lower it and try again. When he backs up even with just one paw reward him! This exercise needs to be done in very small increments, and it will be a while before you can back him up for a meter or more.

2.3 Leash Walking

Sooner or later, you're going to want to take your puppy out for a walk, and in this case, sooner is better than later. If you're not up to speed with vaccines yet, feel free to take him for walks on isolated streets, through empty fields, through your friend's yards, or anywhere else you can! But take him on a walk for sure.

The general rule is that you would walk a puppy in a harness for a minimum of six months before starting to use a collar. Many people choose to use a harness forever, and that's perfectly fine. Whatever you decide to do, the puppy has to learn how to walk politely before you can even consider putting him in a collar, otherwise, you risk him getting injured.

There are two kinds of puppies. The first kind feels the leash attach to them and plop down on the ground, refusing to move at all. The second kind tears off exploring the second you open the door and spend 100% of their time at the very end of the leash. Both of these situations and everything in between is perfectly normal and nothing to worry about.

For puppies that refuse to move, all you need is patience. It seems like it will last forever, but in reality, it's only a phase that is sure to pass sooner or later. The important thing is that you put the harness on your puppy daily, and try to have fun and play with him. Toss some treats on the ground and see if that will get him moving. If it doesn't, no problem! Try again the next day. If you always make it a fun game, you can be sure that sooner or later your puppy will take to his harness and leash.

The more common option is that your puppy will want to explore his surroundings and will be yanking you left and right every time you're out for a walk. This is also completely normal. Puppies tend to be very curious and this is their chance to understand the world. While some training at this point is essential, don't expect to have a polite leash-walker until your puppy becomes an adult.

The best thing you can do is fill your pockets with treats and toys before going out on your walks. Don't discourage your puppy from exploring, as this is an important part of socialization. However, periodically, call him back. Get his attention with a sharp noise (or his name, if you've done the exercise from the previous chapter!) And reward him heavily when he looks at you. This will be much harder to do while out on the street than it is in the house, so be prepared to take it slowly and invest in superior quality treats. Don't bother calling him just as a squirrel is passing by, it's unreasonable to expect that kind of concentration from a puppy.

A regular walk with a young puppy (before six months of age) should follow these steps:

1. Putting on the harness and leash. Try not to take ages with this step as it will agitate your puppy. If the harness is complicated, practice on a toy until you can do it in one or two smooth motions.

2. Waiting until the puppy calms down. If he likes walks, chances are he's going to be jumping up and down like a little maniac at this point. Under no circumstances start the walk until he settles down. Wait as long as it takes.

3. Go out into the street. Look for quiet, remote places. Avoid major distractions and scares such as trucks passing by, dogs barking from behind fences, etc.

4. Let the puppy roam a little. It's better, at this point, to have a slightly longer leash that allows him to sniff around rather than a short one that he will reach the end of in no time. Under no circumstances should you use a retractable leash. They teach puppies to pull!

5. When he gets close to the end of the leash, call him back. For some puppies, this may be after one step, for others, it takes a while. When he comes back, reward him heavily.

6. Take one or two steps with your puppy next to you. Remember the technique called "luring"? Keep treats in your hand and use his nose as a magnet to walk side by side. Reward him after a few steps.

7. Let him roam again. Repeat steps 4 to 7 throughout your walk. Don't let the puppy place himself at the end of the leash and mush like a Husky. The more he does it, the harder it will be to correct.

The other useful trick most puppy parents could benefit from is an exercise called "You're a tree". With particularly excitable puppies, they may need extra help understanding that the end of the leash is not where you want them to be, and that fun things don't happen there.

The way you set up this information is by freezing and pretending to be a tree every time the leash is pulled tight. When your puppy discovers that the fun has stopped and he can't move forward anymore, he will turn around and look at you. For some puppies, this can take a while, but be resilient. Never ever give in to your puppy pulling, no matter how desperately he is trying to reach something. After a few seconds, if he still isn't looking at you, start taking a few slow steps in the opposite direction to where he is pulling. Our goal is to teach him that as long as the leash is tight, he doesn't get what he wants. When he finally relents and puts some slack in the leash, reward him with an epic puppy party and lots of treats. The grander your rewards are at first, the faster he will learn.

Sometimes, it can seem like a frustrating uphill battle while you're teaching your puppy to walk on a leash. For many months, it's possible that you will only be able to take a step or two in "luring" before he gets distracted. You will look like the world's most indecisive walker, stopping dead every few steps and walking backward one time out of two. You have to persevere! Walking a leash puller can be a nightmare, and dangerous for both you and your dog. With perseverance, they can turn into a happy and relaxing experience.

On your walks, there are a few mechanical aspects you should keep in mind. Of course, hot tarmac and delicate puppy paws don't go together, and you should try walking on grass or dirt as much as possible in the summer. It's also a great idea to carry water with you for both yourself and your pup.

Surprisingly, winter comes with its own perils. Ice can be painful to walk on, but puppy pads are decently protected against the cold if you don't over-do it. However, the salt that we humans use on roads in order to prevent icing is much worse. Walking on salt can be very damaging for young paws, especially if you don't wash them off carefully as soon as you get home. While some people choose to buy dog boots, they're actually awkward to use and not that comfortable for your pup. A much better investment is a tin of good quality pet Paw Balm.

2.4 Socialization

Part of the reason why you want to take your puppy out on regular walks is for exercise. The other part is socialization. You may have heard this word a lot, however, lots of people are confused about what it means because it reminds you of humans "socializing". So it must be allowing your puppy to hang out with other dogs, preferably at the dog park, right?

Not at all. Socialization does include other dogs, but they are only a very small element. When your puppy comes into the world, he's pretty much a blank slate. He needs to spend the next six months of his life figuring out what is "normal" and what is "danger".

Socialization is the process by which you teach him to distinguish between these two states.

Lots of literature will give complicated explanations about socialization, imprinting, fear periods, and the various concepts that fall under this category. That's all well and good, but they don't concern you as the owner of a 2 to 6-month-old puppy. You need to know how to handle the practical side of things simply and with confidence.

The most important socialization effort you need to make for your puppy is to consider all of the possible things that your adult dog may run into throughout his whole life. Some of these are easy to guess: cars, large animals, small animals, storms, umbrellas, masks, children, fences. Write down a list of the most important ones. Others may depend on your specific living conditions: Do you garden? Do you have strange tools and machinery in the garage? Do you have funny people over all the time? Do you foster pets? Do you have farm animals? Do you go to a lot of outdoor concerts? Do you take the bus or train a lot?

For the first six months of your puppy's life with you, the most important thing you can possibly do is take him from place to place, from event to event, and from person to person, and show him that all of these things fall under "normal" and not "danger".

It's called a "socialization window" because, like a real window, it closes. Once your pup is about 8 months old, anything he's never seen and doesn't know how to handle can and will be treated as "danger". To some dogs, this may mean being nervous, shy or frightened. To others, it might be a call to arms.

Most puppy owners socialize badly in two major ways. One common version is that of the excessively confident puppy parent which simply throws her dog in a dog park and hopes for the best. This doesn't actually help with socializing, because once your puppy has met a couple of dogs and got the idea, anything beyond that isn't "socializing" anymore. It can also foster bad play habits, or a fear of other dogs if they suffer a traumatic experience while at the park. You have little control and that's not ideal.

The other version is that of the overly-protective parent. They try to "socialize" their puppy while holding him in their arms the entire time. Whenever the puppy gets frightened or shy, they pick them up and walk away. Whenever the puppy growls, they pick them up and walk away. The problem with this kind of attitude is that it reinforces your dog's belief that something is "dangerous". You picked him up, therefore he was right – it was a dangerous situation. Phew.

Unless you're actually in a dangerous situation, that can have serious consequences. You don't want to teach your dog to be afraid every time a car passes by, a dog sniffs her, or another puppy play-growls. In most situations, it's better to be close to your puppy, but allow her to explore life naturally and normally without stressing her out. Calmly carry on with what you're doing and she will pick up the cues and stay calm too.

When socializing, try to hit these major points, but be sure to add your own:

- Family members, neighbors, friends, and their pets

- Strangers around town and their dogs

- Cars, bikes, trucks, etc. passing by

- Being in the car, going for a drive

- Being on public transport

- Funny noises like people dragging things on the ground or loud engines

- Sunglasses, hoods, hats, umbrellas, masks

- People and dogs running or playing sports

- People having a loud argument

- Strange smells like gas stations or food markets

- Climbing into objects such as boxes, on top of objects such as benches, going around objects such as concrete posts, going through tunnels or narrow passageways

- Climbing stairs

- Walking on metal grates, concrete, leaves, sand, grass

- Having a leash, harness and collar put on daily

- Being touched, being handled, going to the vet, going to the groomer

- Being brushed and washed

- Any time anyone says "My dog is scared of" make a note and prevent the same thing happening to your dog!

This socialization window is a strange and fun period for both owner and puppy. You should find yourself often going out of your way to meet strangers, investigate strange noises, and do strange things. You will often find yourself giving your dog treats while other people are talking to you or even petting him. You should also allow strange people to give him treats (which you supply). The good news is that most people love puppies and this will be a lot easier than it sounds.

What happens if your puppy has a negative experience during his socialization window? This is something we want to avoid at all costs. A simple negative experience such as a child pulling his tail painfully while you're distracted for one second can turn into a lifelong habit of running from, or worse, attacking children. You should exert control at all times so that interaction with new things happens under your terms. If something unwanted happens, it will be your job to focus on replacing that one negative experience with a hundred good ones.

2.5 Grooming

It may seem strange, but the first part of learning how to groom your puppy actually coincides with part of his socialization! It's important to let her know that being touched is a normal part of being a puppy. This includes sensitive areas such as paws, tail, belly, mouth, and ears. You also have to introduce water, the tub, the brush, and the nail clippers slowly. You won't be able to get much grooming done before this step!

Grooming needs change from breed to breed and from dog to dog, but there are a few unavoidable steps for all dog owners. The major ones are fur care, nail care, and oral hygiene. Getting your puppy accustomed to being groomed is an essential part of your daily activities.

Oral Hygiene

It's a good idea to start practicing this early and frequently because it can be a sensitive moment for many dogs. Most dogs won't automatically allow you to touch their face, let alone open their mouth, but it's your job as a caring parent to slowly show your puppy that there's nothing to be scared of.

On the first day, this would probably only be light touches close to the face followed by rewards. If it seems your puppy is particularly easygoing, touching the face directly and rewarding is still fine.

By the end of the first week, you should build up to putting your hands around the puppy's snout for a second, gently and without any pressure, and rewarding heavily when he lets you do it.

By the end of two weeks, you want to be able to lift his lips gently without causing him any stress and without putting much pressure on his lips. This is a good time to take a look at his baby teeth and keep an eye on any permanent teeth that might be coming along!

By the end of the first month, you should be able to use a finger brush specifically designed for brushing puppy teeth to clean his teeth for a few seconds. Toothpaste is not as important to them as it is to us, and the simple mechanical process of brushing should be more than enough. Don't add any unnecessary discomfort at this point by doing it for more than a few seconds at a time or by adding strange tastes to the equation.

Once your puppy is comfortable with having his teeth brushed, you can fall into a regular rhythm of brushing depending on his needs. This should, ideally, happen every few days.

Nail cutting

Nail cutting can be very tricky, and many pet owners choose to have their pet's nails cut professionally. It doesn't have to be frightening however. Most of the time, cutting nails at home is less stressful and traumatic for your dog. All you need is a good quality dog nail clipper – accept no substitute! Absolutely do not use human clippers for this job.

Your goal at first will be to touch your puppy's paws daily and get him comfortable with that. Reward him after every time you touch his paws so that he makes a positive, happy association with that gesture. Do it during happy, playful moments and don't extend the time or the level of pressure until he's comfortable.

When touching his paws becomes a normal, day-to-day activity, try picking him up and holding his paws in your hands for a few seconds. Reward him for any increase in tolerance, and don't overdo it. When you can gently squeeze a paw for a few seconds with no problems, start touching the nail clippers to your puppy's nails. If he seems startled by the sensation, that's perfectly normal. Take a step back and ease him into it.

If he's fine with it, you can start by clipping just the very tips of his nails. If you're lucky and have a white nailed pup, you should be able to see that inside his white nail there's a pink center called a "quick". Ideally, you should cut in such a way that you never risk touching this pink area, as that would be extremely painful for your pup. If it does happen, be sure to put some styptic powder on the nail, and don't try to clip his nails again for a while.

If your puppy has black nails, it will be harder to tell and you have to be even more careful. Special nail clippers with infrared sensors exist, or you can clip off thin slices until you start to see a white center to the nail. Look up images online for clipping black dog nails and you will have a good reference point.

Fur care

When it comes to caring for your puppy's fur, you will need to research what specific needs his breed has. Each type of brush is better suited to certain types of fur, so make sure you get the right ones. Brushing your puppy should start off in the same way as everything else: first, get him used to the motions and tools involved. Pet him frequently, and try using a microfiber cloth of glove before moving on to a brush. Since brushing is pleasant, most puppies take to it quickly.

Bathing, on the other hand, is where most puppies get hung up. If you rush this process, you risk having a dog that is afraid of the bathtub for life, so be careful. Before washing your pup, get him accustomed to all of the individual elements of bath time separately: the empty tub, the smell of the soap, the feeling of the towel, running water near him, running water on him. Only when he seems comfortable with all of these should you put them together into one single event. Try to keep baths as quick and simple as possible, at first, and don't be ashamed of keeping treats and chews by the tub to occasionally encourage him.

You should take care to buy a bottle of all-natural dog shampoo that is suitable for your individual dog's skin and coat. Try to read the ingredients list and make an investment in a natural, hypoallergenic brand. You won't be using large quantities of it, so you might as well spring for the superior shampoo.

Thoroughly rinse your pet's fur, and if you repeat the shampoo (according to the instructions on the bottle) be sure to rinse well the second time around too. When drying your dog, it's better to use towels and let him shake it off whenever it's warm enough. If you use a hairdryer, it has to be either designed specifically for dogs or set on a "cool air" setting. Your puppy will also know what to do: one good shake will get most of the water out of his fur and onto your walls, so hang out in the bathroom for a little bit.

No matter what you do, chances are you're going to get dog hair around the house and on your clothes. Breeds with shorter hair tend to shed more than breeds with long hair, but all dogs shed to some extent. Regular brushing with the right brush and bathing help with this problem to some extent, however, they don't cure it completely. It may be better to simply be prepared and buy a few rolls of sticky hair-removing tape for your clothing and couch.

Other puppy care tips

It's a good idea to keep a close eye on your pup's eyes, nose and ears at all times. Look inside the ears, and if needed, clean them with a soft cotton cloth every now and then. Take note of any particular discharge coming from these areas, and ask your veterinarian if you have any doubts or concerns.

When it comes to outerwear, use your judgment. Dogs that are well-suited for cooler climates and have nice thick fur don't need jackets and are only going to suffer while wearing them. A Husky in a coat is a recipe for overheating. Most hunting and sporting dogs are sturdy and waterproof and will do just fine without clothing. If your dog has very short fur, then it might be time to buy them a nice sweater for Christmas. Smaller companion dogs such as the

Chihuahua often need a jacket to get them through the winter. In the case of short-haired dogs, use your common sense. If it's cold for you, it's cold for them too.

2.6 Nutrition

Your puppy is going to spend the first year of his life converting whatever food you give him into strong muscles and bones. The quality and quantity of the food you provide for him in this period are absolutely essential. While not all budgets are created equal, you're not really saving money if you're going to spend it all on veterinary bills in the near future.

When planning his diet, take into consideration that he will only need a good quality dry food, treats and rewards, chewy things, and freshwater. Dogs don't need wet food the way cats do, so it's better to take that money and invest it in premium quality kibble. Some very good brands can be found online and deliver to your doorstep, and there are offers and solutions for every budget.

When you first get your puppy, they will have been eating a specific brand of food at the breeder or shelter. Find out what that brand is and get a bag since you can't abruptly switch over to a new food. A newly-adopted puppy has plenty of frightening things to worry about and doesn't need the added problem of indigestion. Start mixing in your brand of choice after a few days, slowly increasing the quantity until his diet is made up entirely of what you intend to feed him until he becomes an adult.

You should feed puppies puppy-specific food until they are fully grown, however, breed specific food is not necessary and often less nutritious than other varieties. You can recognize good quality dog food by learning to read labels. Don't fall for packaging that claims it's "healthy", "organic", "natural" etc. Those words don't mean anything. All you need to know is in the ingredients list.

Whatever food you pick should absolutely NOT have:

- corn and wheat gluten
- artificial coloring or flavors
- meat and grain meals and by-products
- anything other than meat as a first ingredient

Ideally, the ingredients list should contain:

- real meat as a first ingredient
- named animals and organs, nor just generic "meat product"
- rice or peas as the carbohydrate

- a high protein content (ideally over 30%)

Veterinarians often recommend a specific brand, but you don't necessarily have to take that as a definitive answer. Most of the times, they are sponsored by that brand. Most dog food bags will come with instructions on serving quantities depending on your puppy's breed, age and weight, however, these are more often than not exaggerated. A much better indicator of how much your puppy needs to eat is checking out breeder websites and each breed's caloric requirements.

Puppies should ideally be fed two to three times a day. You can expect them to need a bathroom break within 15 minutes after each feeding if everything is going well. Under no circumstances should you leave food out for your puppy all the time. Meal times and quantities should be fixed, and the bowl should be emptied within a few minutes. If your puppy is leaving food in the bowl, then there is something wrong. Either he doesn't like the food, he is feeling sick, or you are over-feeding.

The best way to know whether you're giving your puppy the right amount of food is to examine him. Look at a short haired breed or touch a long haired one to see if you can feel his ribs. You're supposed to be able to feel them with your fingers, but not see them. Your puppy is going to look chubby, but as he grows into an adolescent dog he should have a visible waistline. He should maintain this waistline throughout his life. A dog that is straight all the way from his shoulders to his pelvis is overweight.

It's very easy to lose track of how much we are feeding our puppies, especially during their first few months of life, because they get so many rewards and treats. For some small breeds which only eat under 100 grams per meal, this can easily make a significant impact. You have to always take care to feed less when you treat more, and should even consider using all of his kibble allocation for the day as treats and rewards. Hand-feeding during training sessions is a wonderful bonding experience between you and your pup. At any rate, don't think that you can get away with giving him treats on top of his regular meals.

Having fresh clean water available at all times is of the utmost importance. Puppies get very easily dehydrated, especially in the summer, while playing and running around. Early signs of puppy dehydration are dry and sticky gums and tongue. In a normal state, his gums and tongue should be wet. Another easy way to tell he's dehydrated is if the skin on his back and shoulders don't spring right back after being gently pulled up.

It's fine to remove the water bowl after dinner, however, and set it back down before breakfast. If we drink a large amount of water before going to bed, we need to get up at night. It's the same for our puppy, and we want him to sleep through the night as soon as possible.

If your puppy is eating a complete and balanced diet you have no reason to worry about supplements. Adding vitamins and minerals can actually upset the balance in his body and be harmful to his growth. Supplements are not something you should ever consider without a specific recommendation from your vet.

Part 3. Preventing and Correcting problems

Let's face it, puppies are awful. They grow up to become amazing, wonderful dogs, however when they're young they can feel like a complete disaster. It sometimes seems like they chew everything they see, chase everything they see, and pee on everything they see. There's no such thing as a trouble-free puppy. Bringing a dog into your life and home is a massive responsibility and that decision should not be taken lightly.

In an ideal world, when we bring a puppy home, we will be able to remember all of the instructions we ever read, we will never make a mistake and our puppy will be perfect. In the real world, however, that never happens. Real life gets in the way of even the most well-meaning of training schedules. Mistakes happen, family members have conflicting ideas of what "educated" means and plans go out the window.

Puppies who are misbehaving are never doing it on purpose. They aren't capable of evil, that's one of the reasons why we love them. Every dog does every single action fully convinced that he's doing the right thing. Even when a frightened dog bites a person, they're just doing what they learned was right: defending themselves. There's absolutely no cause to ever get angry at a dog, and no excuse for letting them suffer when we could help them understand the world.

Since we are the ones to blame for their mistakes, it's only fair that we should know how to set things right when they go wrong. Prevention is ideal, but even if the damage is already done, there is always a way to make things better for both you and your dog.

3.1 Redirecting, Reinforcing, Exercising

The three most important techniques you need to know as a pet parent are redirecting, reinforcing, and the power of exercise. If you understand the concept of these, you can adapt them to any situation and any problem you may be having with your puppy.

Redirecting

Many first-time puppy owners don't realize that scolding your puppy almost never works. It's very rare that they will actually understand what they are being scolded for. Even if they do, chances are they will develop negative associations with you as well as with that situation.

So what are you supposed to do when you catch your puppy in the act of doing something bad? The best option possible is to calmly but firmly remove him from the problem and redirect him onto the appropriate version of that activity. Then you reward him for doing the right thing.

If you catch him chewing slippers, you take away the slipper calmly and replace it with a delicious chew bone. You are redirecting him to the appropriate toy. If he would rather chew slippers, then you're not making his chew bones appealing enough – feel free to cheat and dip them in sodium-free chicken broth, rub them all over with a slice of hot-dog, or any other trick you can think of that will make them smell nice.

If you catch him about to pee on the carpet, you calmly take him outside and redirect him to the appropriate potty area. When he does use it, reward him. If he's pulling desperately on the leash to get to a squirrel, back away a good distance and redirect him onto some amazing toys and treats that are even more interesting than the squirrel.

Redirecting can be a powerful tool and it can be used in almost any situation. It should be your automatic answer whenever your dog is doing something he shouldn't be doing. That is why you should always keep his treats, toys, and chews within reach and even take some with you on walks.

Reinforcing

Unlike redirecting, which is our automatic answer whenever our puppy does something bad, reinforcing is our automatic answer whenever he does something good. It's not enough to keep telling him what not to do – you can't expect him to read a book or play chess. You need to also give him options of what to do and express your approval when he does them.

Reinforcing is what we've been doing every single time we rewarded our puppy's good behavior. He does something, we are happy about it, we reward him, and that behavior gets reinforced as being good behavior. Reinforcing doesn't happen overnight, and one treat doesn't make an obedient puppy. But each time he does something and it has a positive outcome, he's a little more likely to do that same thing again.

You already know about reinforcing your puppy when he goes potty in the correct place, or when he performs "sit" or "down" for you. But there are hundreds of situations throughout a normal day in which you can take advantage of what your puppy is naturally doing in order to reinforce it. Think about what you would ideally want your dog to be like, and work towards constructing that kind of behavior.

Some of the best things to reinforce by rewarding:

- Whenever he goes calmly and happily to nap on his bed. Yes, even if it disturbs him.

- Whenever he meets somebody new and approaches them confidently but calmly

- Whenever he sits close to you. Whenever he follows you and pays attention to you.

- Whenever he brings you something. This is important if you ever want to teach him to play fetch.

- Whenever he doesn't react badly to a scary situation, such as a loud noise.

- Whenever he is chewing on his own toys

- Whenever he refrains from chasing the cat.

There are hundreds of other situations, depending on what your home life looks like. Find the ones that are important to you and reinforce positive behavior.

While reinforcing can be a great thing, you also have to be very careful with it. It's easy to accidentally reinforce bad behaviors by allowing them to be rewarded. For example, every time your dog jumps on you and you give him a cuddle, you are reinforcing him jumping on people. Think about how that may feel to strangers, children, or the elderly. Be very careful what behavior you chose to reinforce.

Exercising

The most important tool in your arsenal for bad behavior prevention is exercise. It holds true that a tired puppy is a happy puppy, but even more so that a tired puppy doesn't have the energy to get into trouble. Sporting and hunting breeds, in particular, tend to have a lot of energy, but so do many other dogs. Infamous breeds that will make you exercise way more than you ever planned include: Border Collie, Jack Russell terrier and most other Terriers, Labradors and Golden Retrievers, German Shepherds, Husky dogs, and many others.

Puppies have even more energy than their adult counterparts, so it stands to reason that the only way you can ensure a few hours of peace and quiet is by providing them with vigorous exercise. The fun thing about puppies is that their exercise requirements take three forms, and all three of these forms have to be fulfilled: physical, mental and social.

Letting a puppy run around in a large yard may give him a chance to stretch his legs, but won't actually do much in the way of keeping him calm and satisfied because there are no mental or social elements to that exercise. Similarly, doing lots of obedience sessions in a day may be exhausting, but he will still need a chance to run and stretch his legs.

The best day for a puppy includes a nice long walk, which is physically tiring but also gives you a chance to practice obedience and to socialize. Playing with you at home is also important. Tug of war is always a favorite game for puppies as it releases a lot of tension and is quite tiring. Playing fetch is great, but won't substitute for walks and interaction as it isn't very mentally stimulating.

You should include short training sessions, as well as the chance to play with other people or animals. On a day that includes all of these activities, you can be pretty sure that your puppy won't get bored and get into mischief.

It's important to keep in mind, however, that puppies are still growing. Their muscles and bones aren't fully developed, and some types of exercise can create serious problems. Most notably, jumping is not something that you should encourage until after your puppy has stopped growing. Walks and tug of war are generally safe for all breeds. Some breeds, like those with shorter snouts, will have a harder time with physical exercise and should focus more on mental stimulation. Talk to your vet about what the limitations for your particular puppy should be.

The other important thing to remember is that getting two dogs and hoping they will play with each other isn't going to get you off the hook when it comes to exercise. They might, but it won't fulfill their needs at all. Puppies need regular interaction with humans and lots of dogs to be happy, as well as walks and obedience training. Getting two puppies will be double the responsibility and take twice as much effort to educate, so don't rush into that decision.

3.2 Unwanted biting and chewing

We've spoken a little bit about unwanted chewing in our section on redirection, but we need to take a closer look at this very common puppy problem. When you get your puppy, most likely he will have two rows of needle-sharp tiny teeth. Their teeth are insanely sharp to make up for the fact that they don't have as much strength in their jaw.

Most puppies are going to use their teeth in two major ways: to chew things, and to chew your hands. This behavior is perfectly normal, but you do have to keep it under control. It's your job to make sure that the objects being chewed are the right ones, and that his play-biting doesn't get out of hand.

When it comes to chewing, you should invest in a variety of puppy-appropriate chew toys to keep his mouth busy, particularly during that terrible teething stage in which it seems that their mouth is never empty. Puppies would rather chew on softer objects at first, like your slippers or the pillow, and it's hard to get them to let go. Things that smell like you are going to be particularly interesting.

If you want to keep up with his curious mouth, you can't expect to just throw toys on the ground and let him have at them. That may work for some pups, but not for most. Here's a list of tricks that you can use to make chew toys more appealing:

- Offer a variety of textures from soft to durable

- Dunk them in sodium-free chicken broth

- Store them in his kibble bag

- Rub them with delicious treats

- Fill them with food – especially the Kong

- Keep them in your pocket for a while

- Use them as toys if they are soft enough. Toss them, tug them, make them move.

The more he chews on his own toys, the more the habit gets reinforced, the more he is likely to do it again. Find a way to get the ball rolling.

It's not a good idea to provide puppies with stuffed toys. While stuffed animals are cute for us, they will become just another chew toy to the puppy. Tearing up and destroying a stuffed animal is actually very pleasant, so once they get a taste for it you can expect them to do the same to your pillows. It's also not a good idea to use squeaky toys. Most of the time these contain small parts that could be easily swallowed. Shop around and look at your options before making a decision.

Kong puppy toys are very popular. They are rubbery cones which are hollow on the inside, allowing you to stuff food and treats in there. Puppies have to work out how to get the food out by chewing, rolling, dropping and licking the toy. These toys are an amazing resource because they can keep your puppy occupied for a long time. Many parents feed their puppies entirely from Kong toys for the first few months in order to provide extra mental stimulation and exercise. You can fill them with anything, including their regular kibble, and you can even pop them in the freezer for a cool treat that will soothe the aching gums of a teething pup.

Play biting is a whole other matter. While chewing is a soothing, calming activity, play biting is exciting and fun for your puppy. All puppies are mouthy, and all puppies grow out of it – with the right care.

In most cases, stopping puppy biting is a two-step process. The first step is making it clear that you don't like it, and the second step is offering an alternative. When puppies play with each other and things get a little too rough, they yelp. That usually gets everyone to stop what they are doing. Similarly, when your puppy gets too rough on your hands, giving out a loud "ouch" should be enough to make them stop for a second.

Use that second wisely! Have either a tug toy or treats handy at all times, and redirect mouthy behavior into obedience training or a game of tug. Continue to redirect every time it happens, and reward your puppy for choosing to chew on his toys or play tug instead of attacking your hands.

Some puppies have a stronger prey drive than others. That's the impulse that makes them want to attack anything that moves and keep attacking it until it stops moving. The fox terrier, for example, is brave and tough enough to take down an angry badger. You can believe that a puppy of these breeds is not going to back away just because you said "ouch".

In that case, you will need to use the time-out rule. The rule is that every time your puppy bites your hands too hard – and it's up to you to decide how much is acceptable, "gentle" biting and what crosses over the line – you have to pick him up and put him in a one-minute time-out. This can be either in a room, a playpen or a crate. It's possible that he will complain and bark, in which case you can't let him out until he settles down – you don't want to reinforce barking and whining.

This time-out rule has to be strict and happen every time, otherwise, it won't mean anything to your puppy. When you let him out, propose a game of tug of war. If he still insists on going after your feet or hands, put him in time-out again. The reason why time-out is very important for puppies with high prey drive is that they get so excited they simply can't be reasoned with anymore. A brief time-out will help calm them down.

There are signs that will let you know if your puppy is one of the highly excitable, high-prey drive pups that benefit from time-outs. Usually, they won't even flinch no matter how loudly you yell "ouch". Sometimes they may even get more riled up and go after your hands and feet even more. Usually, once they start attacking your feet it becomes impossible to distract them even with treats or toys. If you have a puppy who is willing to ignore a delicious treat, then it's clear that he's overexcited and needs a little timeout.

3.3 Chasing

The history of our beloved pets is quite interesting. Their jobs ranged from protector to hunter to loving companion, and they were bred to do those jobs to perfection. They all come from the same common ancestor, however, and that ancestor is a hunter.

When we talk about a specific breed's prey drive, we talk about the natural instinct that makes that breed want to catch a moving object and the tenacity with which they will pursue it. Prey drive is what makes a dog jump up and chase a ball, cat or bird. Prey drive is also what makes them nibble at your heels when they're overexcited and you're moving.

A dog with low prey drive may not feel like getting up from his comfortable spot in the sun just to chase a ball. He is also a lot less likely to be mad at passing birds, chase other pets around the house, or get excited as soon as you pick up a toy. It's potentially a great thing, depending on what you want from your dog.

A dog with high prey drive is going to become an expert at fetching the ball and catching a Frisbee in the air. He is well suited for lots of games, but he's also very likely to annoy other pets, fixate on squirrels and birds, and kill any small animals in his part. This type of dog isn't even recommended for households that have small pets like parrots or guinea pigs, however, they can be amazing sports companions.

No matter what kind of dog you end up with, there are situations in which you don't want him to chase everything that moves. It's always hard to keep a balance between discouraging unwanted chasing but not discouraging participation in chasing games. Scolding or punishing a dog for chasing can easily end up suppressing his prey drive, and if he's sensitive that may mean he will never play ball with you. It doesn't sound like a tragedy, but handling an energetic dog without the benefit of fetch, Frisbee, tug of war or lure chasing is an absolute nightmare.

Most commonly, people complain about unwanted chasing in two major situations: during walks, and at home with other pets. There are plenty of other possible instances where it might happen, but the same solutions would apply. Keep in mind, however, that to some extent all puppies chase and there's no stopping them completely. Nor should you, it is a normal healthy instinct of any dog. Training them not to chase pigeons isn't an excuse for letting them off the leash near a busy street. There are some stimuli that even the most well-behaved dog won't be able to resist. Leashes are there for a reason.

When you're out with your dog, potential chase hazards include birds, cats, other dogs, squirrels, leaves, and anything else that moves. If you're unlucky, small children running around could easily fall under this category.

The trick is not to throw your dog in the deep end of the pool all of a sudden. You have to teach him to resist temptation slowly. Ideally, practice his leash walking and keeping his attention on you for a long time on empty streets with no distractions. Then, repeat those same exercises within view of moving objects, but not closer. Then, when your puppy is comfortable paying attention to you while there are kids running or bicycles in sight, move a little closer to them. As soon as he starts to give in to that impulse to chase, step back a few meters to where he has more control and practice again. Keep his attention on you with treats and toys and make slow progress towards your target.

It will take months of keeping him attentive within sight of chase triggers before you can go near them. This is not a fast process. Your goal is to be able to walk with your dog through a crowded street without him tugging towards other dogs, kids or birds, but it can take years to build up to that. The self-control exercise we will be discussing shortly also helps with this.

When it comes to at-home shenanigans, it may be a little harder to keep things in hand. You don't always have a handy leash to pull him back from distractions, and he's not always paying attention to you. So when the cat or a bike or the postman pass by, it's fair game. This can be a serious problem, particularly for the other pets in your household. You need to help your puppy practice self-restraint, as well as teach him the "leave it" command. The following exercise does both and is very important. You should never underestimate the power of self-restraint for a dog.

Leave it

Do you remember the reward and punishment exercise from the beginning of this book? If not, now is a good time to check it out and start working on it, because it is the basis of this exercise.

If you have done your homework, then by now you should be able to hold a treat in your fist and have your puppy leave it alone and wait patiently for you to open it and give it to them. It's time to build on that and work up to one of the most amazing commands you can ever teach your dog, which is "leave it".

Get down on the floor. Put a treat in your hand and close your fist over it. Make sure your puppy knows it's there. Put your closed fist in front of him. He should know the trick by now and wait patiently.

Instead of saying "Yes" and letting him have the treat, open your fist slowly. As soon as he makes a move for the treat, close it again. When he stops, open it slowly again. It should take a few tries before you get to open your fist all the way with your puppy still waiting patiently. Don't keep him waiting for long! As soon as he doesn't immediately lunge for the treat, say "Yes" and reward him heavily.

Repeat this many times, and once it looks like he gets the idea, as you open your fist, add the command "leave it". Slowly, over many days, increase the time you take before saying "yes" to a few seconds. If you say "leave it" and the puppy lunges for the treat, close your fist, calmly say "no" and try again. If he seems frustrated, take a break and next time shorten the wait times.

Keep repeating this until he knows what you expect of him. Then, after saying "leave it", very slowly place the treat on the ground. Give him half a second of waiting time and say "yes", at which point he should lunge for it. Slowly increase the duration of the exercise. Be sure to do this in short sessions over many days!

When your puppy is comfortable leaving the treat on the ground for a few seconds, and he has more or less understood the concept of "leave it", the real fun begins. Start by gently rolling the treat on the ground in front of him while he waits for it. Progress to flicking it a few centimeters away from him. Progress to tossing it across the room. Work your way up, slowly as always, to being able to say "leave it" and tossing the treat across the room from standing height. Be sure to take your time to make sure every single step is nailed down before you move on to the next one. If your puppy gets up to chase the treat, you have failed by moving to fast. Next time, be sure to make it so easy for him that he can't possibly make a mistake again. Don't ever give him the chance to get it wrong twice in a row.

Once you get good at the "leave it" game, practice it outside. Try it with a ball or tug toy. Bring treats with you wherever you go, and work on "leave it" whenever you can: on the street, in queues, at restaurants. The more you do it, the better your chances that it will sink in. Soon, you will be able to drop a chicken leg in the kitchen, shout "leave it" and pick it back up without your dog snatching it! That kind of self-control takes a long time and a lot of practice.

The great thing about this exercise is that once "leave it" becomes a part of your puppy's vocabulary, you can use it to stop him chasing the cat, birds, or anything else. Remember to work your way up to the harder ones slowly, and reward him a great deal every time he obeys you. "Leave it" can be a lifesaving tool that prevents your dog from eating a dropped pill, a mushroom in the woods, or a decaying corpse. It can prevent him from dashing across the road to chase a cat. It can save his life in so many ways that it's fully worth the time and effort.

2.4 Aggression and reading body language

When people think of "aggression" in relation to dogs, they often imagine that an "aggressive" dog is a bad dog. There is a great difference between aggression in general and unwanted aggression, but they have one thing in common: in neither case is the dog to blame.

Dogs can become aggressive for many reasons. It often happens to dogs that were deprived of proper socialization in their youth, or dogs who experienced a traumatic event and now react aggressively because they are afraid. An adult dog that has a serious unwanted aggression problem is going to need the help of a professional behaviorist, and you should seek their guidance and counsel before trying anything by yourself.

All puppies have a certain level of aggression. It's a natural trait in all animals and is a good and healthy element of their personality. Aggression is what makes him play tug of war with you, or guard the house for you. It may save his life in a dangerous situation. There's nothing wrong with a normal amount of well-controlled aggression. However, we want to prevent those seeds from sprouting into full-blown trees of unwanted aggression problems.

The first step in preventing unwanted aggression is being able to identify it. Lots of websites and books like to give out helpful charts or photos showing various dog positions and telling you what emotion each position means. You need to understand one thing right now: none of that is true. While some gestures and motions can sometimes indicate certain emotions, there is absolutely no guarantee that that's the case. Each dog is different. Some breeds trick you on purpose. You can never rely on body language in a potentially dangerous situation with an unknown dog. You have been warned.

Often you will be told that a dog wagging his tail is friendly. This terrible advice is usually given to children and puts them in the most danger. The reality is that almost all dogs wag their tails when they are friendly, but some will also do it when they are agitated, excited, or angry. Brave harrier breeds like terriers can often get so excited about chasing and killing something that they will wag their tails. That's not something you should bet your safety on.

A dog that has his tail between his legs is usually nervous or frightened, that is true. However, fear in dogs can manifest in many ways. They may freeze, they may feel better if you approach them and comfort them, or they may decide to defend themselves. The great majority of cases of unwanted aggression towards humans stem from fear, so a tail between the legs on an unknown dog should be a warning sign.

We also always imagine that a dog who is about to attack you will be growling, snarling, snapping and have the hair raised on the back of their heads. For many dogs that is not the case. Infamously, Rottweilers can look perfectly calm until the very last second. However, if they do have raised hairs going down their back, then you can be sure it's trouble.

The point is that the only reliable body language you can be sure to recognize is the one that belongs to your individual puppy, by observing him over many months and knowing how he reacts in different situations. Only experience can help you understand what your puppy is saying with his body.

When it comes to puppies, "unwanted aggression" can take many shapes, but you will know it when you see it. Here are some very common signs that you might have an unusually aggressive pup:

- He growls to defend his toys or food

- He goes for your hands and feet when he's excited

- He doesn't quit no matter what treats you offer

- He fixates on certain situations which always trigger him

- He freezes and stares at you when you reach for his bowl or blanket

- He nips at you when you try to touch him or wake him up

These situations are all unnerving, especially if they happen repeatedly. Many puppy owners have lost their temper because they experienced one or all of these. It's crucial that you don't respond to aggressive behavior with more aggressive behavior, as that can have wild and unexpected consequences.

The first thing you should do is check in with your veterinarian and make sure that everything is fine. A lot of puppies who are sick or in pain will react aggressively, so if he suddenly starts to show this kind of behavior, look out for any other symptoms of illness. If you've ruled that out, here are some other things you can do:

- Redirect him. Just like in our explanation on redirection, you will need to have some other outlet on hand for him to vent his aggression. It's a good idea, especially if you have excitable puppies, to stash tug ropes all over the house. That way, whenever he wants to take it out on you, he can take it out on a rope instead.

- Put him in time-out. If there's no stopping him, a short time-out to cool off is the only thing you can do. Don't make these time-outs long, they aren't an excuse for you to go away and ignore your puppy for hours. A few minutes tops should do it, then if he comes out just as excited, put him back for a few minutes more. Be sure to place him in time-out calmly and gently.

- Keep him in a harness and leash, even around the house, during moments which you know will trigger him. If he goes crazy every time your kids get home from school, for example, that would be a great time to keep him in check using a leash. Take it off again when the moment passes.

These are immediate responses that you can use in case of trouble, however, there are many more things that you can do in order to prevent this kind of trouble from showing up at all. First on your list should be providing for adequate exercise and mental stimulation for your puppy. A tired puppy is a happy puppy. Don't give him the chance to have spare energy to burn at the end of the day, because it's very likely that he will burn it in unfortunate ways.

Sometimes, as is the case for small children, being excessively tired can also cause puppies to be grumpy and angry. You may notice, for example, that when you get home from a very long walk he gets agitated and starts biting your heels as soon as you reach the door. He may have a bout of inexplicable, crazy running in the yard or through the rooms. These are classic signs of a tired pup. Thankfully, the very simple and effective cure for that is to put him in his crate for a nap. When they get that tired, you can expect them to sleep it off for at least an hour or two!

Teaching your pup basic obedience commands either by yourself or by going to an educator can be invaluable. It's not just about having the ability to say "sit" and have your pup sit. That may work, and it may interrupt his aggressive behavior. But more importantly, it creates a bond between the two of you that will improve your understanding of each other.

Similarly, spending time playing and having fun with your pup will also strengthen that bond. The more he plays with you – tug, fetch, hide and seek – the more he will understand you and what your rules and limits are. You can initiate play and stop it whenever it gets too rough or you get tired. You can show him that you're a fun person to be around as long as he plays nicely. By simply playing, you will be teaching him more than you can imagine.

Another very important effort in preventing unwanted aggression in adult dogs is proper socialization as puppies. We've spoken about socialization previously, but the specific area of it that helps prevent aggression problems is intraspecies socialization. That means interacting, from an early age, with other dogs. The reason why this is important is that dogs have ways of transmitting messages to each other that we can't even fathom. It's not just a growl or body language, it's scent and chemical reactions as well.

When a puppy interacts with an adult dog, for example, the adult dog will automatically take a dominant position in their relationship. He will allow the puppy to play and even play-bite, but if it gets out of hand the adult dog can easily stop him and make it very clear why. Whereas you can stop the puppy, but will always struggle to explain the "why" to him. When playing with each other, puppies have their own system. Even though to us it looks like a painful mess of teeth and claws, they are following instinctive rules which you wouldn't be able to impose. When one puppy bites too hard, the other emits a piercing squeak and leaves the game. Puppies that insist on biting too hard or playing too rough eventually get ostracized and have nobody to play with, so they quickly learn to stay within the limits.

In order to reap the benefits of this kind of socialization, you need to get it done in the right context. A dog park is your worst nightmare because you have no control over who goes in it and what goes on there. A much better option would be a group puppy training class. You should also organize play dates with other friendly puppies or adult dogs, as well as attend dog-friendly events or parties. Great socialization sessions should last long enough for the dogs to play to their satisfaction, but not so long that they grow tired and grumpy. Depending on your dog, this can mean anything from ten minutes to two hours.

While passing other dogs in the street and greeting them is always a fun puppy activity, that won't count much towards preventing aggressive behavior since there just isn't enough time for them to interact and communicate.

While we're on the topic of meeting other dogs on the street, let's talk about puppies who have excessive aggressive reactions towards other dogs while on a leash. To some extent, it's normal that not all dogs will get along with all other dogs. Some puppies are just sweet and good-natured and will make friends easily, and pet owners are often deluded into thinking that this would, or should, be the case for all dogs. It's actually far more common that dogs will not always make friends, especially within the same gender, and almost never in the case of unneutered males. We need to put our expectations aside, and instead settle for them tolerating or ignoring other dogs.

In order to achieve this, make sure you don't put your puppy under undue stress during your walks. If you tense up when you're about to meet a new dog, so will he. Dogs can feel out emotions and there's no way to hide, so try to stay relaxed. Don't ever pressure them to meet or spend time with a dog if they don't seem happy to, and don't allow them to spend time with dogs which are rude or aggressive themselves. If things get heated, never scold or violently tug at your dog. While that may stop him at the moment, it won't produce any lasting educational benefits. Instead, keep calm and keep walking.

Unless you specifically have a reason for wanting your puppy to interact with another dog, it's perfectly fine to pass by calmly without greeting them. In fact, you should practice keeping your puppy's attention on you while other dogs are passing by. It's much better to offer controlled interaction with dogs that you know and trust rather than allow your puppy to insist on meeting every single dog on the street.

One of the most important things to keep in mind when it comes to preventing puppies from turning into aggressive dogs is that you can't be aggressive with them. No matter how frustrating it can be, shouting, hitting or shaking your dog is only going to make the situation worse and has never fixed any problems. At most, your dog will fear you, and he will behave, but you will have no relationship at all. You want your dog to look at you as a wise leader, not a frightening jailer.

Finally, if none of these tips seem to work, don't hesitate to contact your local canine education center and ask for help. Unwanted aggression in dogs is not something to toy with, and nothing can compare to expert help and advice. A good education center can even help you improve the situation for adult dogs which have deeply rooted problems, so a puppy should be no worry at all. Remember that all progress is made over time, in incremental steps. Don't believe any well-intended advice from people who think they have the instant cure to aggression problems.

3.5 Shy, reactive, and fearful dogs

One of the greatest difficulty for a new puppy parent can be having to care for a shy, reactive and fearful dog. It's always a shock when you expect to have crazy adventures with your canine pal and instead, you find him jumping at every shadow. And while some dogs end up having reactivity problems because of a lack of socialization or traumatic experiences, it's also completely possible that you got a puppy who is naturally shy and reactive. It's not his fault, it's just who he is.

Recognizing symptoms of a reactive puppy early is key. As you take your daily walks, take note if he seems to jump at the sight of people and dogs, if he growls at them or if he tries to back away. Pay attention to how he reacts around dark shadows, tunnels, moving objects, wind, or any other potential trigger. Spotting a fearful dog isn't hard, he will probably make it very clear to you, but just to make sure you know what you're looking at here are the classic signs:

- Excessive licking of the lips

- Ears flat and set back

- Tail down, between the legs. Rear end curved

- The whole spine curved

- Usually positioned sideways respective to the object of his fear

- Low growling

While it can be sad and disheartening to see that tail constantly between his legs, those ears constantly flat, and that back constantly arched, don't panic. There are many ways in which you can help a fearful, reactive puppy reach a greater level of calm and confidence. there's no reason why, through education and care, he can't end up having a perfectly normal and healthy life!

The first thing you need to do is teach your dog a very fun game called "look at it". This very simple game is going to quickly turn things around for your reactive pup. Here's how it works:

Look at it

Take a walk with your dog near an area where you know they might have a lot of triggers, such as a large park. Find yourself a comfortable spot somewhere far away from everyone else, but just far enough that you can still see them.

Settle down comfortable and wait for some people or dogs to pass by – whatever it is that triggers him. As soon as he looks at one – don't even wait one second, your timing has to be perfect – tell him "yes" and give him a treat. Feel free to substitute "yes" for "good boy" or a clicker if that's what you're using. At first, your dog won't know what to make of it, but he will be happy for the treat.

He will look back towards the frightening thing. Say "yes" and give him a reward. Every time he looks at something scary, the very next instant you have to be there to reward him. Slowly, over time, this is going to affect a major shift in your dog – instead of being frightened, he is going to be cautious but happy because he knows a treat is coming. You are doing something called "counter-conditioning", or changing his negative association with an event or object into a positive one. The frightening experience becomes a game to him.

Over time, after many repetitions and many days, you will notice that your dog looks at something that scares him, and then immediately looks back towards you expecting his reward. This is a major milestone. Celebrate!

Confidence gaining for fearful dogs

Once you start working on counter-conditioning those reactions, you should also build up your puppy's confidence in parallel. A confident puppy is going to have far less of a problem walking down the street, and with enough confidence, his fear issues could disappear entirely.

The first step is to help him gain confidence by having a period of time in which nothing frightening happens. You have to break the cycle before healing can begin, and there are many things you can do to help:

- avoid crowds and strange dogs

- use your body to act as a shield between your dog and frightening things

- use a crate when strangers come to visit

- use quiet and deserted streets for your walks

- don't be shy in telling people not to approach you or your dog

Try to keep your puppy calm and happy in any way you can without reinforcing his fears that the world is a big bad place.

Always let your dog set the pace. This holds true for all puppies, but especially fearful ones. Be patient and listen to them. They will make it clear when they're not ready for a certain situation or encounter – don't push them. They need to build confidence in themselves and they won't do that by constantly being in uncomfortable situations. More importantly, they need to have faith in you and know that you will care for them.

The next step in confidence building is playing games. One of the most therapeutic games for a dog is tug-of-war. Playing tug-of-war with you gives them a great workout, but also strengthens their bond with you, heightens their natural instincts and builds their self-confidence. If you play it right, you can teach your dog a great number of things by playing tug. So how do you do it?

Tug-of-war

Start off with a rag, or something soft and easy to bite. Keep in mind that the mouth of a young puppy is quite small. Get down on the floor in a room with no distractions and start gently moving the rag about left and right and playing with it yourself. When your puppy starts to be interested, move it away from him to encourage his chasing instincts. Most puppies will take to this game instantly and bite the rag, pulling on it. With some, it takes longer. Make sure there is nothing distracting or frightening them and persevere! If they seem fearful, try to tie the rag to a string and stand further away from your puppy.

When your puppy gets the rag in his mouth, keep it moving. Moving targets are interesting, still ones are not. The moment you stop moving it, he will start chewing it or let it go entirely. Move it in such a way that if he tries to chew it, he loses it! When you see that he has a good solid grip and is holding on tightly, let him win. Show him that he is brave and strong by pretending that he beat you every now and then.

This would also be a good opportunity to teach your puppy the command "drop it". It's another bonus to playing tug-of-war, and a great command to have on hand when you need to get something your dog is holding in his mouth. Besides, every new chance you get to understand each other better is valuable!

To teach "drop it" start by playing tug. When your puppy has a firm grip on the toy, move your hands so that they are quite close to his mouth and there's not much toy visible. The trick is to then stop the toy completely. One good way to do this is to put your hands (with the toy) in your lap. Your puppy will give one or two tugs, trying to figure out why the toy is no longer moving. Say "drop it" and wait. Sometimes it takes seconds, sometimes minutes, but if you keep that toy completely immobile, sooner or later he will let go and look at you. That's when you should say "yes" and immediately start playing again.

The more you repeat this, the faster he will get at letting go of the toy on command. It's a very easy trick, and one too few puppy parents teach.

One final thought on shy, reactive and fearful dogs: never punish them for being afraid. You're going to make matters much worse very quickly, and there's no point. Kindness and love will take you much further down the road of understanding than anger will.

3.6 Separation anxiety

Before we talk about how to prevent and deal with separation anxiety, let's take a moment to make sure that we are all on the same page when it comes to what separation anxiety actually means. There are many things which look like separation anxiety but aren't, and your dog may very well be suffering from one of these.

What separation anxiety is

Separation anxiety is when your dog is in extreme distress from the moment you leave until the moment you return. No matter what you do, he won't calm down. Leaving him a pound of steak or the most delicious bone in the world on the floor wouldn't distract him. The company of another pet wouldn't distract him. Not even being exhausted from a five-hour walk would help – he needs to be close to you and that's it. As you can see, in reality, when people think they're dealing with separation anxiety, they almost never are. So what other things look like separation anxiety and how can we fix them?

The most common answer is boredom. In 99% of cases where puppy owners think it's separation anxiety, it's really just boredom. A bored puppy, when left alone, will find something to entertain himself with. He will bark, howl, or whine the entire time. He will chew up the furniture. He will pee on your shoes. In some extreme cases, they can easily get so agitated as to chew on their own feet or tail to the point of drawing blood. It can seem absolutely gruesome... and yet it's just boredom.

So how do you test if that's the case? Easy. Leave a hunk of steak in the room with him and leave the house for ten minutes. When you come back, is the steak gone? Then it's probably not separation anxiety. A dog suffering from anxiety would never be able to settle down and eat.

If boredom is the problem, the answer is simple but usually unpleasant for new puppy parents. You need to spend more time exercising your dog. You need to give him physical exercise by way of fetch and tug, mental exercise by way of obedience training, and stimulating new things to interact with by way of walks. There's no way around it, so you might as well accept it: puppies take a lot of time. Set up a healthy routine, consider leaving him alone in a controlled environment where he can't do damage and leave him with a Kong or other puzzle toy to keep him busy. Don't forget the chew toys!

So let's say you tried the "hunk of steak" test and he didn't eat it. Does that mean that he's suffering from separation anxiety? Maybe not. There's still another option to consider. It's possible that your dog isn't suffering from separation anxiety but from a similar issue called "isolation anxiety". Isolation anxiety is when a dog has an issue with being left alone. It's not about you personally, it's just about being deprived of all stimuli. So how can you test if what you're dealing with is isolation anxiety? Easy. Leave the house, but leave your dog with another person or dog for ten minutes. If he's still equally agitated, it's separation anxiety – he can't be separated from you. If he's fine, it's probably just about isolation.

A dog that has trouble handling isolation can be helped in several ways. The obvious solution is to make sure he's not isolated when you go away. Having another person stop by frequently to play with him would help, as would having the company of other pets. In many cases, even just having entertainment makes a difference: a window to look out of and see people passing by, a TV left on the animal channel, a radio left on soothing music. Combining this with the previous advice for boredom should do the trick. A well-exercised puppy which is tired and happy is less likely to suffer from isolation anxiety as well.

If you've eliminated all of the other options, then perhaps the only one you're left with is separation anxiety. Often, separation anxiety will have all of the symptoms of boredom and isolation anxiety, but with a few added behaviors:

- nervous pacing as you prepare to leave

- whining and trembling

- howling the entire time you're gone

- nervous licking of the lips and excessive salivation

- desperate attempts to escape confinement, often resulting in heavy property damage and injury to your dog.

What causes separation anxiety?

Separation anxiety is not "bad behavior" since the dog has no control over his reaction whatsoever. In that sense, it's much more similar to human depression than anything else. And much like human depression, the causes can often be obscure and varied.

Some puppies are simply more prone to suffering from separation anxiety than others. They are born that way. They will form a strong attachment and dependence to you quickly and struggle to let go of it. There's nothing you can do to identify puppies that have this problem before it actually manifests itself.

Sometimes dogs that come from shelters have this problem. Being abandoned once can have lasting traumatic effects on a dog. Puppies that are never left alone during their first few months of life can develop this problem. Puppies that are left alone too much, or too abruptly can also suffer from it. Or a puppy can experience all of these things, and yet never have separation anxiety.

What can you do about separation anxiety?

Understand that there is no quick fix for this problem. There's no solution that will immediately "fix" your dog, so be wary of taking friendly advice from people who claim that. Start by putting into practice all of the other advice mentioned under "boredom" and "isolation anxiety". Depending on your individual dog, many of those things will help and at the very least they can't hurt. Always start working on separation anxiety problems with a well-exercised, tired dog.

1. Desensitization

At the moment, your dog is very sensitive to your leaving the house. We need to start by making him less so through a process of "desensitization". This implies replacing at least some of his fears with positive emotions. If he begins to get agitated whenever you put on your shoes, try putting on your shoes a couple of times a day without leaving the house. Put them on, and then give him a delicious treat instead. Then take them off and go on with your day. Repeat that many times a day, for many days, until putting on your shoes makes him happy instead of upset. Do the same thing for any action that starts to agitate him. Try to give him an extra special treat just as you're about to walk out the door – something truly irresistible, preferably on an empty stomach. It's perfectly fine to have your dog skip a meal in preparation for receiving something delicious when you leave the house. While you should always try to keep his feeding times regular, separation anxiety is a serious problem and warrants some serious measures.

2. Countering excessive attachment

It's a great thing to have a close bond with your dog, but you're not doing him any favors by encouraging his excessively clingy behavior. Try to be relaxed around him and keep him busy when you're in the house. Get him used to not always being in the same room as you, even if you have to start with only a minute at a time. Get used to resisting his incessant requests for attention. It's cute when you're working at your desk and he puts his head on your knee, but if you cuddle him at that moment you may just be reinforcing his separation anxiety. Avoid getting emotional whenever you leave the house or return home; treat it instead like a completely relaxed situation. Don't even greet your dog before leaving or when you get home. Greeting him enthusiastically as soon as you get home may reinforce his anxieties. Take your time, settle down, and when he's calmer go in for a scratch.

3. Crate training

On top of every other good reason to crate train, it can also help with separation anxiety. A tired, well-exercised puppy that's put in his crate is much more likely to calmly chew his toys or nap when you are away. Think about what it's like for people suffering from anxiety: having the ability to pace nervously, looking out the window every two seconds to see who is coming, or running around fretting is often only going to make you feel more anxious. Certainly, pacing has never helped anyone calm down. It's better to not give your puppy the option to fall into these self-perpetuating, anxiety-inducing habits. A crate will also keep him safer, just make sure it's solidly constructed and well shut. Be sure to check whether your dog actually feels safer and calmer in the crate, as the opposite effect has been known to happen to certain dogs.

4. Other aides

Supplements and homeopathic treatments can sometimes help with the healing process if taken in combination with other helpful techniques described in this chapter. Check with your vet before you give your dog any supplements.

Medication is also an option, but it should really only be a last resort option. Even if your veterinarian is willing to prescribe it, remember that we live in a very Prozac-happy era. Don't go there unless you've tried everything else first.

Some people swear by calming pheromone diffusers. It's very hard to gather statistics on separation anxiety, so there's no guaranteed irrefutable proof that they work at all. Check out the reviews, try them for yourself and see what the results are, if any.

Even more commonly, people recommend the ThunderShirt. This is a canine garment designed to help with dogs who are afraid of loud thunder and other noises, but it seems to have a calming effect that can extend to many other situations such as visits to the vet or being left home alone. This is another product that you can't be sure about until you try it on your dog. Many swear it has miraculous effects, though, so it's worth considering.

Finally, remember that separation anxiety is a tough issue to treat. It may not even be possible for you to improve the situation by yourself, and if that is the case you shouldn't hesitate to talk to a canine behaviorist or a veterinarian and ask for their help. There's no shame in needing expert advice for a serious problem, just don't wait too long to ask for it.

Final thoughts

Having a puppy enter your life changes everything. It will be a roller-coaster of emotions from beginning to end. You may end up suffering from every single hardship known to puppy kind, or you may sail through the experience with no problems. It's important to remember that no matter how hard it gets, neither you nor your puppy is "broken" or "bad" and no problem is so great that you can't work on it. Through persistence, patience, and help from professionals, even the most stubborn dog can become an obedient, loving pet. Don't give up on them and yourself.

Lots of puppies end up abandoned at the shelter because of many of the problems described in this book. In almost all of the cases, all it would have taken to turn the situation around is a little patience, love, and willingness to put in the time. There's one thing you can be sure of, though: you will be rewarded for the effort that you put in with love, companionship, and adventures.

CPSIA information can be obtained
at www.ICGtesting.com
Printed in the USA
LVHW081314260122
709466LV00010B/236

9 781925 992243